LATIN
A Fresh Approach Book 2

By
MIKE SEIGEL
Headmaster of Rokeby School,
Kingston-upon-Thames

Wimbledon Publishing Company

ISBN 1 898855 26 9

Dedicated to the Very Highest Quality in Education

LATIN – A Fresh Approach Book 2
Mike Seigel
LIBRARY OF QUALITY IN EDUCATION

First Published in Great Britain in 2000 by
WIMBLEDON PUBLISHING COMPANY LIMITED
P.O. BOX 9779
London SW19 7QA
Fax 020 8944 0825

ISBN 1 898855 26 9

Produced in Great Britain
Typesetting by Dave Allery
Illustrations by A. Harrison
Cover Design by Malvinder S. Soor, P.M. Graphics

MIKE SEIGEL

Mike Seigel has had a distinguised academic and teaching career. An Oxford University graduate, he won an Exhibition to New College where he read Classics. After joining St Paul's School and Colet Court in 1973, Mike was Head of Classics at Colet Court from 1976 to 1987, during which period more than 80 of his pupils suceeded in getting scholarships to the most prestigious Independent schools in the UK, including Eton, St Paul's Winchester and Westminster. He then concentrated his teaching on GCSE and A level classes, as well as working as a Careers and Universities adviser, before being appointed Headmaster of Rokeby School, Kingston-upon-Thames in 1999.

Mike Seigel is married with two children. His outside interests include travel, cinema, theatre and swimming.

FOR

Wendy, Emma and Alexander

*and all my pupils
past, present and future*

Acknowledgements

The author and publishers are grateful to the following for permission to reproduce copyright material and illustrations:

David Camden, Leo Curran, Barnaby's Picture Gallery, Paula Chabot, Leslie Noles, John Traupman, Barbara McManus

Every effort has been made to contact all copyright holders before publications. If there are any omissions the publishers will be pleased to rectify them at the earliest opportunity.

Introduction

I am delighted to be introducing the second book in the three volume
series which will make a complete beginner's course in Latin. This book
continues the philosophy and practice of Book 1, with a variety of exercises
to meet the advancing needs of the students, while grammar and
vocabulary are again brought in at a pace designed to suit the pupils.

There continues to be a balance between the language and the culture of
Ancient Rome, with background material aimed at both general interest as
well as the Common Entrance syllabus.

Once again I hope that this book will make Latin a pleasure rather than a
chore, and that it will be enjoyed by pupils and teachers alike!

MKS June 2000

Contents

REVISION OF NOUNS

1

In the previous book we met nouns of the first two groups, which we call **Declensions**.

Nouns like **puella** belong to what we call the **First Declension**; nouns like **servus, puer** and **ager** to the **Second Declension**.

If you are at all unsure of these, use the tables below to refresh your memory.

	SINGULAR	PLURAL
NOM	puell**a**	puell**ae**
VOC	puell**a**	puell**ae**
ACC	puell**am**	puell**ās**
GEN	puell**ae**	puell**ārum**
DAT	puell**ae**	puell**īs**
ABL	puell**ā**	puell**īs**

	SINGULAR	PLURAL
NOM	serv**us**	serv**ī**
VOC	serv**e**	serv**ī**
ACC	serv**um**	serv**ōs**
GEN	serv**ī**	serv**ōrum**
DAT	serv**ō**	serv**īs**
ABL	serv**ō**	serv**īs**

	SINGULAR	PLURAL
N/V	puer	puerī
ACC	puer**um**	puer**ōs**
GEN	puerī	puer**ōrum**
DAT	puerō	puerīs
ABL	puerō	puerīs

	SINGULAR	PLURAL
N/V	ager	agrī
ACC	agr**um**	agr**ōs**
GEN	agrī	agr**ōrum**
DAT	agrō	agrīs
ABL	agrō	agrīs

Now is perhaps also a good time to revise the case uses which you have so far learnt:

NOMINATIVE is used to describe the Subject of a sentence:

> **puellae** ambulant
> **The girls** are walking

VOCATIVE is used to address people and is sometimes preceded by the word "o":

> **(o) puellae**, ubi estis?
> **Girls**, where are you?

ACCUSATIVE is used a) as the Object of the sentence:

> **puellas** videmus
> We see **the girls**

b) after certain prepositions:

> **ad puellas** ambulamus
> We walk **towards the girls**

GENITIVE is used to denote possession:

> **puellarum** libros habeo
> I have **the girls'** books

DATIVE is used a) as the Indirect Object, often after verbs of giving, showing etc.:

> **puellis** libros do
> I give the books **to the girls**

or
> I give **the girls** the books

b) to denote advantage (or disadvantage!):

> cenam **puellis** paro
> I am preparing dinner **for the girls**

ABLATIVE is used after certain prepositions:

> **cum puellis** ambulamus
> We are walking **with the girls**

Here are some new nouns to be learnt before you do the exercises in this chapter:

Like **puella:**

luna	moon
mora	delay
porta	gate
terra	land, ground
turba	crowd
umbra	shade
unda	wave

Like **servus:**

oculus	eye
socius	ally
somnus	sleep

and some new prepositions:

ante + Acc	before, in front of
post + Acc	after, behind
sine + Abl	without
sub + Acc/Abl	under
trans + Acc	across

EXERCISE 1.1

1. pueri in hortum sine mora festinant.
2. luna viam nautis fessis monstrat.
3. cur ante portas statis, puellae?
4. Marcus turbam amicorum videt.
5. regina sub umbra cum filia sedet.
6. agricolae trans agros ambulant.
7. post cenam servi in culina manent.
8. socii ad muros appropinquant.
9. num undas times, Gai?
10. vir pecuniam post casam celat.

EXERCISE 1.2

1. The farmers are hurrying towards the gates.
2. The little girl is waiting behind the house.
3. Marcus is walking in the garden without Julia.
4. The great waves are destroying the shore of the island.
5. Why are you not sitting under the shade, Marcus?

Note these other uses of the DATIVE and ABLATIVE cases:

DATIVE a) as the Direct Object after a few verbs such as **pareo** (I obey) **placeo** (I please):

puellis paremus
We obey **the girls**

b) to denote possession:

puellis est casa nova
The girls have a new house
(lit. there is a new house to/for the girls)

ABLATIVE to describe how something is done:

puellae **hastis** pugnant
The girls are fighting **with spears**

EXERCISE 1.3

1. nonne magistro paretis, pueri?
2. casa nova agricolae placet.
3. dea oculos nautarum somno superat.
4. socii hastis et sagittis pugnant.
5. puero est equus magnus.
6. cur liber novus pueris non placet?
7. Marcus amicum prope portas videt.
8. turba puellarum Marcum in horto exspectat.
9. nonne luna nautis terram monstrat?
10. servo misero non sunt duo oculi.

EXERCISE 1.4

Before translating the following sentences, copy out each one, underline each noun and say what case it is.

1. servi cenam pueris parant.
2. magister pueros ira terret.
3. turba puerorum post murum manet.
4. cur ante casam amici sedes, Marce?
5. puella e casa in hortum sine mora festinat.
6. in horto cum amicis sedemus.
7. poeta pecuniam puellis saepe dat.
8. num pueri hastis in agris pugnant?
9. dea ex undis in oram ambulat.
10. luna viam pueris monstrat.

When translating into Latin you need to take great care over the word **"with"**

e.g.   I attack the house **with arrows**

tells you how I attack it and so **"with arrows"** requires the **plain Ablative**

          casam **sagittis** oppugno

BUT   I attack the house **with my friends**

means   **"together with"** and so requires **"cum"**

          casam **cum amicis** oppugno

EXERCISE 1.5

1. We are walking towards the gate with our* friends.
2. The schoolmaster frightens the small boy with his* anger.
3. Surely the girls are not fighting with spears?
4. The slaves always obey the farmer.
5. Marcus has a new book.

* Remember that these words do not need to be translated.

EXERCISE 1.6

Write two or three Latin sentences to describe what is happening in the picture below.

EXERCISE 1.7

1. Explain the meaning of the following English words, and show how they derive from Latin:

    association   somnolent   subterranean   umbrella.

2. Find English derivations from the following Latin words, and write a sentence for each which clearly shows its meaning:

    ager   hortus   luna   oculus.

LEGENDS OF ROME

You read towards the end of the last book about **Romulus and Remus**. This was a story which children living in Rome at the time of **Julius Caesar** would have heard and read. In fact most of the stories which come down to us about the very early period of Rome's history were written by a man called **Livy** who lived and wrote at the time of the first emperor **Augustus** in the opening years of the first millennium.

To Livy and the people of his time these stories were very popular and Livy retold them in such a way as to excite the Romans of his time with grand tales of long ago. In rather the same way you may have read about King Arthur and the Knights of the Round Table, stories designed to entertain but which may owe more to fiction and imagination than to fact. These can therefore be described as legends, rather than history.

Livy described his work as a history, but much of what he writes in his early books can certainly be thought of more as legends. Several of these tales will be told in the following chapters.

When **Romulus** founded the city of Rome, it was extremely small – more like a village by modern standards. But when Livy was writing it was a thriving, cosmopolitan centre much more like a modern city, and had a population of about one million.

Population was a problem for the very first Romans, and in particular there were not enough women. Livy tells us that the neighbours of the new city were unwilling to allow their women to marry the Romans. Romulus therefore invited his neighbours to a festival, and on the appointed day crowds flocked into Rome, many out of curiosity to see the new town.

When the show began, the young Romans at a given signal burst through the crowd and seized the young women. Most of the girls were the prize of whoever got hold of them first, but some who were especially beautiful were taken to the homes of leading citizens.

This act of violence, not surprisingly, put an end to the fun of the festival. The parents escaped and planned their revenge. Romulus tried to reassure them, but the neighbours wanted war, and were led by the tribe of **Sabines.**

There might have been terrible bloodshed, but the women soon got over their annoyance, and enjoyed the attention of their Roman captors. Time passed and they had babies. So when the battle started, the Sabine women walked between the angry fighters and implored them not to fight as they were now related! "We are mothers now," said the women, "we do not want our husbands or fathers to die on our account. Think of your children and your grandchildren!"

This unexpected intervention of the women is said to have stopped the battle and put an end to the war. Romulus now had enough families to develop his new city, and is said to have divided the population into groups according to the names of the Sabine women.

EXERCISE 1.8

1. Do you think that the story of the Sabine Women is likely to have happened? Give reasons for your answer.

2. Romulus was the first of seven kings to rule Rome during this early period. Find out the names of the other six and make a complete list.

3. What legends can you think of besides King Arthur from Britain's early history? Find out about one, and describe it to the rest of your class.

THIRD DECLENSION NOUNS 2

Nouns that are classed as **"Third Declension"** originate from slightly different groups and are therefore a little more difficult to learn. The **Nominative Case** can have a variety of endings, and it is therefore essential to learn the stem of these nouns as well.

You did meet a few of these nouns in the previous book – like **rex** (king) and **mater** (mother).

Now look carefully at how they decline:

	SINGULAR	PLURAL
NOM/VOC	rex	reg**ēs**
ACC	reg**em**	reg**ēs**
GEN	reg**is**	reg**um**
DAT	reg**ī**	reg**ibus**
ABL	reg**e**	reg**ibus**

	SINGULAR	PLURAL
NOM/VOC	mater	matr**ēs**
ACC	matr**em**	matr**ēs**
GEN	matr**is**	matr**um**
DAT	matr**ī**	matr**ibus**
ABL	matr**e**	matr**ibus**

In order to learn exactly how such nouns decline you will have to learn them with the **Genitive Case**, so that you know the **stem**.

These nouns can be either **Masculine or Feminine**; sometimes you can tell by the meaning as in the nouns above, but many of these nouns you will need to learn with their **gender** as well.

So you would learn

rex, regis (m)	king
mater, matris (f)	mother

Other nouns of this type that you have already met are:

pater, patris (m)	father
frater, fratris (m)	brother
soror, sororis (f)	sister

EXERCISE 2.1

1. puella fratrem in via salutat.
2. soror regis prope ripam natat.
3. pater iratus est, quod pueri matrem non iuvant.
4. pueri cenam patri et matri parant.
5. Marcus cum sorore parva ad casam festinat.
6. cur in horto manes, pater?
7. Iulia est soror Marci.
8. filiae cibum matribus dant.
9. rex cum quattuor fratribus per viam ambulat.
10. Quintus equum novum patri monstrat.

EXERCISE 2.2

1. The girls see their brother in the garden.
2. The slaves are preparing the food for the king.
3. The boy's father is a good man.
4. I am giving money to my sister.
5. Where is the king's daughter?

Other nouns of this type include:

arbor, arboris (f)   tree
clamor, clamoris (m) shout
dux, ducis (m/f)   leader, guide
flos, floris (m)   flower
miles, militis (m/f) soldier
uxor, uxoris (f)   wife
vox, vocis (f)   voice

EXERCISE 2.3

1. milites per viam festinant.
2. pueri matres clamoribus terrent.
3. sunt multae arbores in horto regis.
4. puellae flores pulchros matri dant.
5. pueri voci patris parent.
6. pater villam novam prope arbores aedificat.
7. uxor ducis cibum militibus parat.
8. cur flores deles, o male puer?
9. nuntius regis ducem militum salutat.
10. magister uxorem in culina iuvat.

EXERCISE 2.4

Rewrite the following sentences putting the nouns, verbs and adjectives in the plural, and then translate them into English.

1. puella florem prope arborem videt.
2. miles bonus ducem iuvat.
3. puer fratrem in via oppugnat.
4. dux iratus est, quod miles clamat.
5. vox ducis militem terret.

You will have noticed that in this type of noun the **Nominative & Accusative Plural** have the **same ending**: -ēs

Great care must therefore be taken when translating:

e.g.   **milites** in via stant
            The soldiers are standing in the road

            milites in via videmus
            We see **the soldiers** in the road

Never translate the first word of a Latin sentence before reading the rest of the sentence: as you can see from the above example, the first word may look like the subject but in fact be the object. Be warned!

Here are some more 3rd Declension nouns to learn before doing the next exercises:

canis, canis (m/f)	dog
comes, comitis (m/f)	companion
eques, equitis (m)	cavalryman
iuvenis, iuvenis (m)	young man
mulier, mulieris (f)	woman
sol, solis (m)	sun
senex, senis (m)	old man

EXERCISE 2.5

1. canes per viam festinant.
2. canes in horto spectamus.
3. equites milites ante muros oppugnant.
4. iuvenes in ora cum filia regis videmus.
5. mulieres cibum et aquam senibus parant.
6. cum comitibus per silvam ad ripam ambulo.
7. deus Solis est Apollo.
8. quot iuvenes sub arboribus vides?
9. cur dux equitum hastam parat?
10. clamores canis senem saepe terrent.

EXERCISE 2.6

1. The cavalry are hurrying towards the walls.
2. The young man is walking with his dog into the wood.
3. We are watching the women in the fields.
4. Why are the old men waiting near the trees?
5. The young man's mother is a beautiful woman.

EXERCISE 2.7

mater ante ianuam casae stat et pueros* exspectat. subito Marcum et Iuliam videt.

mater: salvete, pueri. intrate casam.
pueri: salve, mater
mater: hodie non laboro, quod fessa sum.
Marcus: cur cenam non paras? nonne patrem exspectas?

mater: pater in urbe cum comitibus manet.

Iulia: sol est <u>calidus</u>. in casa non laboro.

mater: festinate <u>igitur</u> e casa in hortum et sub arboribus sedete. ego cibum et aquam porto.

Marcus: <u>nunc</u> sub umbra arborum sedemus. fessus sum.

mater: cur fessus es? non laboras, quod hodie non es in ludo.

Marcus: saepe fessus sum. saepe servos in agris iuvo.

mater: nunc non laboramus. fabulam narro.

Iulia: <u>qualem</u> fabulam narras? narra fabulam de mulieribus.

mater: de rege Romulo et mulieribus Sabinis fabulam narro. tacete.

mater fabulam narrat, sed <u>mox</u> somnus oculos puerorum superat.

* remember that	**pueri** often means	children
	calidus	hot
	igitur	therefore
	nunc	now
	qualem (Acc of **qualis**)	what sort of?
	mox	soon

EXERCISE 2.8

1. The children like the shade of the trees.
2. We often help mother in the house.
3. Father is soon tired, because the sun is hot.
4. The women are now sitting under the trees.
5. Why are you not in school today, brother?

EXERCISE 2.9

1. Explain the meaning of the following English words, and show how they derive from Latin:

    canine   fraternal   juvenile   quality.

2. Find English derivations from the following Latin words, and write a sentence for each which clearly shows its meaning:

    flos   miles   rex   vox.

HORATIUS

You read a little more about early Roman history in the last chapter. Legend has it that there were seven kings of Rome, and the last was a man called **Tarquinius Superbus** (Tarquin the Proud). He became so unpopular that he was thrown out of the city, and the Romans decided to elect two **consuls** a year in the hope that no one man would have too much power for too long.

Tarquin fled to a neighbouring king, a man called **Lars Porsena**, and tried to persuade him that in other cities too kings might be thrown out if people saw what had happened in Rome. He therefore pleaded for help from Porsena to regain his kingdom.

Porsena then led an army of **Etruscans** against Rome. The citizens abandoned their farms and retreated into the city. The most vulnerable point of entry at that time was the wooden bridge over the river Tiber. The Etruscan army would have crossed this and forced an entry into the city, had it not been for the courage of one man, **Horatius Cocles**.

Horatius was a brave soldier who was on guard at the bridge that day. He urged his companions to destroy the bridge, while he prepared to hold up the enemy for as long as he could – on his own!

The advancing enemy were amazed at such courage. Two others did stay with him for a while, but he forced them to leave him and seek safety. He challenged the enemy one after another to single combat. At first they hesitated, but then they hurled their spears at the lone figure who stood in their way.

Horatius caught their weapons on his shield and still held his ground on the bridge. The Etruscans then moved forward, and would indeed have pushed him aside by their strength of numbers, but their progress was suddenly checked by the crash of the falling bridge – just in time!

The Etruscans watched in amazement as Horatius, still fully armed, prayed to the god of the Tiber and jumped in. He swam to safety through a barrage of spears aimed at him and reached the other bank where his friends were waiting to receive him.

A legend maybe, but one which became very famous to the Romans and in later time. Have you read the famous poem about Horatius by **Lord Macaulay** which begins …

> Lars Porsena of Clusium
> By the nine gods he swore
> That the great house of Tarquin
> Should suffer wrong no more.

EXERCISE 2.10

Find the poem cited above, read and try to learn some of it. Perhaps your class could learn the whole poem by dividing it into small sections.

MORE THIRD DECLENSION NOUNS

3

Some nouns of this declension have a different ending for the **Genitive Plural**: this ends in **-ium**.

Otherwise they decline exactly like **rex**.

Nouns of this type include:

civis, civis (m/f)	citizen
hostis, hostis (m/f)	enemy
mons, montis (m)	mountain
navis, navis (f)	ship
nox, noctis (f)	night
pons, pontis (m)	bridge
urbs, urbis (f)	city

EXERCISE 3.1

1. cives regem et reginam in via salutant.
2. nox filiam regis non terret.
3. milites fessos iuvamus.
4. decem naves ad oram insulae appropinquant.
5. consul ex urbe cum filio ambulat.
6. cur mulieres in monte alto errant?
7. puellae multos flores ex agris in urbem portant.
8. dux hostium ad montes festinat.
9. canes senem clamoribus terrent.
10. iuvenes puellas in urbe subito oppugnant.

EXERCISE 3.2

1. milites contra hostes pugnant.
2. ad urbem ante noctem appropinquamus.
3. soror poetae sub arbore sedet.

4. dux milites post montes celat.
5. pueri ad ludum sine libris ambulant.
6. cives ante muros urbis stant.
7. cives cum servis in via saepe salutamus.
8. iuvenes trans montes sine duce ambulant.
9. consul urbem sine militibus non intrat.
10. senex noctem nunc timet.

EXERCISE 3.3

Rewrite the following sentences, putting the nouns and verbs into the plural, and then translate them into English.

1. nauta navem parat.
2. iuvenis florem in casam portat.
3. dux trans montem festinat.
4. civis puerum post murum celat.
5. miles cum muliere sub arbore sedet.

Here are a few more 3rd Declension Nouns to be learnt before doing the next exercises:

consul, consulis (m)	consul
custos, custodis (m/f)	guard
gens, gentis (f)*	family, tribe, race
ignis, ignis (m)*	fire
lux, lucis (f)	light
N.B. prima lux	first light, i.e.dawn
tempestas, tempestatis (f)	storm

* **Gen Plural** is **-ium**, and **ignis** usually has **Abl Singular ignī**

EXERCISE 3.4

1. sol lucem nautis dat.
2. tempestas multas naves delet.
3. tres custodes ante ianuam villae stant.
4. consul turbam civium ira terret.
5. duces gentis per silvam festinant.
6. hostes casas civium igni delent.
7. nautae miseri tempestatem timent.

8. hostes urbem ante primam lucem oppugnant.
9. rex multas gentes in urbem novam vocat.
10. Horatius in ponte sine comitibus manet.

EXERCISE 3.5

1. The leader of the soldiers praises his companions.
2. The women are helping the old men.
3. The storm destroys many houses.
4. I am walking towards the city before dawn.
5. The king is approaching without the soldiers.

EXERCISE 3.6

Write two or three Latin sentences to describe what is happening in the picture below.

SCAEVOLA

Another story of the time of Porsena's attack on Rome which appealed to the later Romans was that of **Mucius Scaevola**.

Here again the bravery of one man was held up as an example to follow, and **Livy** includes it in his early history to reflect an age of heroism which he hoped would be repeated in his own time under the **emperor Augustus**.

Augustus

Porsena, the king of the Etruscans, was continuing his siege of the city of Rome, and was hoping that he could starve the poor Romans into submission without actually having to storm it. For the Romans this seemed to be even more shameful than being beaten in battle.

So a young man, called **Gaius Mucius**, asked the senate for permission to cross the river Tiber and to try to enter the enemy lines. This daring man was granted his wish, and he hid a dagger in his clothes before setting off. When he arrived in the Etruscan camp, he mingled with the crowd. It was a busy time as the soldiers were being paid their wages. On a raised platform were sitting two men: one the king, the other his secretary.

Mucius of course did not know which was which, and dared not ask, for this would give him away. So he took his chance, and stabbed – the wrong man! He was immediately seized by the guards and dragged back to the king.

His situation was desperate, but his bravery did not leave him. He boldly admitted that he had come to kill the king, and Porsena angrily ordered him to be burnt alive. Mucius then thrust his right hand into a fire which had already been prepared for a sacrifice and held it there – as if he felt no pain.

Porsena was so astounded at the young man's bravery that he set him free. Mucius then returned to Rome, soon followed by ambassadors from the Etruscan king. Gaius Mucius was rewarded by the senate with lands, and was given the name **Scaevola** – which means "left-handed" – in honour of the brave sacrifice of his right hand.

EXERCISE 3.7

1. Write a brief summary of either the story of Horatius or the story of Scaevola.

2. Which of these two stories do you think better shows the bravery of the early Romans, and why?

3. Can you think of a story in British history where someone thrusts their hand into a fire? Try to find out more about this.

NEUTER NOUNS 4

You have so far learnt nouns that are either **Masculine** or **Feminine**. In Latin there is a third type of nouns which are neither of these, and they are called **Neuter** nouns. (The word **neuter** is the Latin for "neither".)

There are no **Neuter** nouns in the First Declension, but several in the Second Declension: words like **vinum** (wine), **atrium** (hall) or **triclinium** (dining-room) which you met in Book 1.

These decline as follows:

	SINGULAR	PLURAL
NOM/VOC	vin**um**	vin**a**
ACC	vin**um**	vin**a**
GEN	vin**ī**	vin**ōrum**
DAT	vin**ō**	vin**īs**
ABL	vin**ō**	vin**īs**

You will note that the **Nominative and Accusative are the same in both Singular and Plural, and the Nominative and Accusative Plural end in -a.** Both these points apply to **all** Neuter nouns.

You will note that the **Vocative is always the same as the Nominative ending**, and there are not many Neuter nouns that you would find in the Vocative case anyway!

Other nouns like this include:

aurum	gold
bellum	war
caelum	sky, heaven

forum	forum, market-place
oppidum	town
periculum	danger
proelium	battle
templum	temple
theatrum	theatre

EXERCISE 4.1

1. agricola aurum in casa celat.
2. multi cives per vias oppidi ambulant.
3. pericula belli cives terrent.
4. Iuppiter est deus caeli.
5. mulieres ante templum stant.
6. ad forum cum amicis festinamus.
7. pater cum filio in theatro sedet.
8. servi tres lectos in triclinium portant.
9. duo iuvenes in atrio manent.
10. da cibum et vinum militibus, Marce.

Adjectives have always to agree with their nouns (see Book 1, Chapter 15). The adjectives you have so far learnt will have the same endings as the Neuter nouns above.

So	mult**a** templ**a**	many temples
	in theatr**o** nov**o**	in the new theatre

Here are a few more nouns of this type to be learnt before doing the next exercises:

auxilium	help
saxum	rock, stone
verbum	word
arma (pl)	arms, weapons
castra (pl)	camp

EXERCISE 4.2

1. sunt multa templa pulchra in urbe.
2. cives theatrum novum aedificant.
3. milites multa arma ante proelium parant.

4. castra hostium sunt magna.
5. est triclinium pulchrum in villa senis.
6. verba magistri pueros non terrent.
7. auxilium a sociis ante proelium exspectamus.
8. mulieres milites in castris curant.
9. pueri mali agricolae canem saxis oppugnant.
10. Porsena milites verbis iratis terret.

EXERCISE 4.3

1. We are walking towards the forum.
2. There is gold in the farmer's house.
3. The young man gives wine and flowers to the girl.
4. The leader of the enemy does not fear war.
5. The slaves are hurrying into the large dining-room.

There are also **Neuter Nouns** in the **Third Declension**, and you need to learn the following types:

	SINGULAR	PLURAL
NOM/VOC	flumen	flumin**a**
ACC	flumen	flumin**a**
GEN	flumin**is**	flumin**um**
DAT	flumin**ī**	flumin**ibus**
ABL	flumin**e**	flumin**ibus**

	SINGULAR	PLURAL
NOM/VOC	mare	mar**ia**
ACC	mare	mar**ia**
GEN	mar**is**	mar**ium**
DAT	mar**ī**	mar**ibus**
ABL	mar**ī**	mar**ibus**

You will see again that the Nominative and Accusative are always the same, and the NOM/ACC plural ends in -a.

You will see that the first type has endings like **rex** but that the second type is slightly different: **note the ABL SINGULAR ends in -ī and that there is an extra i in the NOM, ACC and GEN PLURAL.**

Because these are **Third Declension Nouns** you will need always to learn them with the **Genitive** (see Chapter 2).

Like	**flumen, fluminis**	river
are	**carmen, carminis**	song, poem
	nomen, nominis	name
	caput, capitis	head
	corpus, corporis	body
	vulnus, vulneris	wound
Like	**mare, maris**	sea
is	**animal, animalis**	animal

EXERCISE 4.4

1. nomen fluminis est Tiberis.
2. multa animalia per silvas errant.
3. iuvenes cum comitibus trans mare navigant.
4. corpus canis in foro videmus.
5. rex carmina poetae laudat.
6. prope flumen sunt castra hostium.
7. clamores animalium pueros terrent.
8. iuvenis in flumine, non in mari, natat.
9. animali est magnum caput.
10. vulnera militum in castris curamus.

EXERCISE 4.5

Before translating the following sentences, copy out each one, underline each noun and say what case it is.

1. verba magistri pueros terrent.
2. puellae ex urbe in agros festinant.
3. delete pontem igni, milites.
4. mulier virum vino superat.
5. servi mensam e triclinio in atrium movent.
6. nuntii cum epistolis in atrio manent.
7. iuvenis animalis clamores timet.
8. clamores mulierum consulem superant.
9. filia regis auxilium nautae dat.
10. nautae oram insulae regi monstrant.

EXERCISE 4.6

1.   The schoolmaster praises the boy's poem.
2.   There is a large body in the sea.
3.   The soldiers are carrying their weapons across the river.
4.   The enemy destroy the camp with rocks.
5.   The old man is walking with his daughter towards the
     bridge.

EXERCISE 4.7

mater et pueri in horto sunt. sol est calidus, et sub arboribus
sedent.

mater: estisne fessi hodie, pueri? fabulam <u>iterum</u> narro.

Marcus: hodie non fessus sum. narra fabulam de militibus,
mater.

Iulia: ego <u>quoque</u> non fessa sum. narra fabulam de feminis,
mater.

mater: fabulamne de mulieribus Sabinis amatis? est fabula <u>et</u>
de feminis <u>et</u> de militibus. Sabini Romanos oppugnant, quod
Romani Sabinorum sorores et filias in urbem portant.

Iulia: feminae bellum non amant, et verba mulierum milites
superant.

Marcus: feminae non <u>semper</u> bonae sunt. narra fabulam de Horatio, mater.

mater: Horatius est custos pontis. hostes Romam oppugnant, sed Horatius pontem delet. itaque urbem servat.

Iulia: narra <u>aliam</u> fabulam de feminis. ego fabulam de Cloelia amo.

mater: Cloelia quoque urbem Romam iuvat. trans flumen Tiberim natat, et rex Etruscorum, nomine Porsena, puellam laudat, quod <u>fortis</u> est.

iterum	again
quoque	also
et ... et	both ... and
semper	always
alius	another, other
fortis	brave

EXERCISE 4.8

1. The soldiers are attacking another bridge.
2. The words of the girls overcome the king.
3. Always help your sister, boys.
4. We praise both mother and daughter.
5. The guards are again destroying the city with fire.

EXERCISE 4.9

1. Explain the meaning of the following English words, and show how they derive from Latin:

   auxiliary   custodian   reiterate   tempestuous

2. Find English derivations from the following Latin words, and write a sentence for each which clearly shows its meaning:

   civis   corpus   hostis   urbs

CLOELIA

Julia – and other girls of her time – might well have liked the story of **Cloelia**. This follows the stories of **Horatius** and **Scaevola**, and does indeed show the courage of women as well as of men. We should probably assume that this story has the basis of truth, for, when **Livy** was writing (two millennia before the days of sexual equality), women did not expect to be involved in the front line of fighting, and this story would have struck them as unusual.

The **Romans** had sent the **Etruscans** certain hostages, and one of them was Cloelia, an unmarried girl. She persuaded a number of other girls who were also hostages to follow her. They managed to escape from the guards and swam safely across the river, although the guards were hurling weapons at them. They thus arrived safely in Rome, and were all restored to their families.

Not surprisingly, **Porsena** was again furious! First Horatius, then Mucius and now Cloelia – a mere girl!! He angrily sent messengers to Rome to demand her return, but then his anger began to fade and he expressed his admiration for Cloelia's masculine courage.

Both sides then acted with honour. The Romans sent her back, in accordance with the treaty they had made with the Etruscans, but Porsena not only protected the brave girl himself, but also praised her publicly. He showed his appreciation of her courageous exploit by allowing her to choose a number of other hostages to be set free with her. She is said to have chosen young boys, and the Romans paid their own tribute to her daring by setting up a statue of her on horseback.

EXERCISE 4.10

1. Do you think that such a story would have appealed to the mainly male audience for whom Livy was writing?

2. Try to find out tales from British history of a young girl carrying out an especially daring deed, and share them with the rest of your class.

3. How do you think you would have reacted in such situations as Horatius, Scaevola and Cloelia? Do you think that their bravery has been exaggerated?

THE PRESENT TENSE: ALL FOUR GROUPS

In Chapter 8 of book 1 you learnt (I hope!) the Present Tense of the first two groups of verbs. Here they are for your convenience and reminder.

Group 1

amo	I love; I am loving
amās	You love; you are loving
amat	He, she, it loves; he, she, it is loving
amāmus	We love; we are loving
amātis	You love; you are loving
amant	They love; they are loving

Group 2

video	I see; I am seeing
vidēs	You see; you are seeing
videt	He, she, it sees; he, she, it is seeing
vidēmus	We see; we are seeing
vidētis	You see; you are seeing
vident	They see; they are seeing

Here are a few more verbs of these two groups for you to learn:

Like **amo**:

neco	I kill
occupo	I seize
oro	I beg
rogo	I ask
vulnero	I wound

Like **video**:

doleo	I am upset
fleo	I weep
iaceo	I lie (down)

EXERCISE 5.1

1.   necatis.
2.   iacemus.
3.   vulnerat.
4.   rogatis.
5.   oramus.
6.   occupant.
7.   flemus.
8.   non dolet.
9.   quid rogas, Iulia?
10. cur fles, Marce?

EXERCISE 5.2

1.   They are killing.
2.   We are upset.
3.   He is asking.
4.   They are wounding.
5.   We are lying down.
6.   She is weeping.
7.   What is he seizing?
8.   Why are you upset, Quintus?
9.   I am not lying down.
10. Surely you are not begging, children?

These groups of verbs are known as **Conjugations**, and there are four of them in Latin.

The 3rd and 4th groups go as follows:

Group 3	**rego**	I rule; I am ruling
	regis	You rule; you are ruling
	regit	He, she, it rules; he, she, it is ruling
	regimus	We rule; we are ruling
	regitis	You rule; you are ruling
	regunt	They rule; they are ruling
Group 4	**audio**	I hear; I am hearing
	audīs	You hear; you are hearing
	audit	He, she, it hears; he, she, it is hearing

audīmus	We hear; we are hearing
audītis	You hear; you are hearing
audiunt	They hear; they are hearing

The endings are the same as for the first and second groups, and are those endings you were encouraged to learn in Chapter 8 of the last book.

However, you will note that the vowel before the endings is different, and note especially the u- before -nt in the "they" ending.

Before doing the next exercises you should learn the following verbs of these two groups:

Like **rego**:

cado	I fall
curro	I run
dico	I say, speak, tell
mitto	I send
pono	I put, place

Like **audio**:

custodio	I guard
dormio	I sleep
invenio	I find
scio	I know
venio	I come

EXERCISE 5.3

1. cadunt.
2. curris.
3. custodimus.
4. venimus.
5. scis.
6. mittimus.
7. invenit.
8. dicit.
9. ponitis.
10. non dormiunt.

EXERCISE 5.4

1.   They are guarding.
2.   He is falling.
3.   She is sending.
4.   We know.
5.   He does not listen.
6.   They say.
7.   We run.
8.   What do they know?
9.   Why are you running, Marcus?
10. Who is coming today?

EXERCISE 5.5

1.   servi cibum et vinum in mensam ponunt.
2.   puer malus in flumen cadit.
3.   senex dormit, quod fessus est.
4.   ad forum cum amicis currimus.
5.   agricola aurum prope silvam invenit.
6.   cur in casam non venitis, pueri?
7.   rex bonus urbem regit.
8.   puer nomen fluminis magistro dicit.
9.   scisne fabulam de mulieribus Sabinis, Iulia?
10. tres viri pontem custodiunt.

EXERCISE 5.6

1.   iuvenes prope flumen iacent et dormiunt.
2.   carmina poetae civibus placent.
3.   mater dolet, quod puer in casam non venit.
4.   puella flet, quod in flumen cadit.
5.   pueri magistro non semper parent.
6.   hostes multos milites in proelio hastis necant.
7.   socii Romanos auxilium orant.
8.   octo servi in triclinium veniunt.
9.   hostes urbem oppugnant, sed non occupant.
10. Gaius regem in castris hostium invenit.

EXERCISE 5.7

1.   I am sending three slaves into the city.
2.   The tired old man is sleeping in the house.
3.   The boy runs and falls into the river.
4.   The young men wound the soldiers with rocks.
5.   The mother is weeping, because she does not find the little girl.

EXERCISE 5.8

Write two or three Latin sentences to describe what is happening in the picture below.

EXERCISE 5.9

Cloelia est in castris hostium cum puellis. puellis dicit.

Cloelia: custodes fessi sunt et mox dormiunt. flumen non spectant. festinate.

puellae: tu es puella fortis. nos quoque venimus.

Cloelia cum puellis e castris ad ripam festinat. custodes puellas non vident. subito puellae in flumine natant. deinde custodes clamores puellarum audiunt. tela in flumen <u>iaciunt</u>, sed puellas

non vulnerant. Cloelia et puellae ad <u>alteram</u> ripam veniunt et
urbem intrant.

in castris hostium rex iratus est et clamat.

Porsena: ubi est Cloelia? cur puellas non videtis, custodes?
custodes: dolemus, quod puellae ad urbem Romam <u>reveniunt</u>.
Porsena: mitte nuntium ad urbem Romam. Cloelia est puella
fortis, sed regi Etruscorum non paret.

telum	weapon
iacio	I throw
alter	the other
revenio	I come back, return

EXERCISE 5.10

1. The guard soon sees the girls in the river.
2. We do not hear the shouts of the king.
3. Why don't you swim to the other bank?
4. The king is angry, because the girls do not obey.
5. The guards wound the messenger with their weapons.

CORIOLANUS

Another famous story from the very early period of Rome's
history is that of **Coriolanus**. It not only appears in the works of
Livy, but also inspired the famous English playwright, **William
Shakespeare**, to write a play about him.

Some twenty or so years after the tales of **Horatius, Scaevola
and Cloelia**, the Romans were still fighting for their existence
against many enemies in the lands surrounding them. One of
these enemy tribes was called the **Volscians,** and a certain Gaius
Marcius earned the extra name of Coriolanus because of his
bravery in storming the Volscian capital of Corioli.

Coriolanus, however, was one of those people whom power
corrupts and he began to behave more in the manner of the
exiled **king Tarquin**. He tried to abuse the new laws of the

Roman people, and was ordered to stand trial. Instead of doing so, he left Rome and took refuge with his former enemies, the Volscians.

The Volscians gave him a warm welcome and encouraged his growing bitterness towards Rome. Coriolanus was bent on revenge against his native city, and war seemed imminent. The Romans sent ambassadors to make terms, but Coriolanus remained obstinate and defiant.

The women of Rome therefore went to see Coriolanus' wife and mother and persuaded them to go, accompanied by Coriolanus' two little sons, into the enemy camp to plead for peace.

When Coriolanus heard that women had arrived to see him, he became all the more determined in his resolve to fight against Rome. He had been moved by the words of neither ambassadors nor priests, and was hardly to be swayed by women's tears!

Coriolanus

One of his companions, however, recognised Coriolanus' aged mother and told him that his mother, wife and sons were there. At last Coriolanus was moved with emotion, and ran to embrace his mother. She, however, was not so easily persuaded by this show of emotion and demanded to know whether she had come to her son or to an enemy. She is said to have made an impassioned speech which melted all Coriolanus' anger and resolve; he embraced his mother, his wife and his sons. He withdrew his army and war was thus averted, but nobody records what happened to Coriolanus afterwards.

EXERCISE 5.11

1. This is a rather different story from the ones in the previous chapters. Why do you think that the story of Coriolanus appealed to the Romans?

2. Find out what other plays from Roman times were written by William Shakespeare. Why do you think that he used Roman stories for his plays in the age of Queen Elizabeth I?

3. With your class write and perform a brief play based on this story.

THE INFINITIVE 6

The Infinitive means **"to do"** something, and in Latin almost always ends in **-re**.

So   amāre   means   **to** love
            vidēre   **to** see
            regere   **to** rule
            audīre   **to** hear

Note how the stem vowel changes according to the conjugation.

One of the few exceptions to the **-re** ending comes with the verb **sum**, whose Infinitive is **esse** (= to be)

The Infinitive is used after certain verbs, some of which you have already met:

e.g.   **amo**   **(1)**   I love, like
            paro   **(1)**   I prepare
            timeo   **(2)**   I am afraid
            scio   **(4)**   I know (how)

So   **natare** timeo   I am afraid **to swim**
            scisne **natare**?   Do you know how **to swim**?

EXERCISE 6.1

1. pueri in flumine natare amant.
2. rex nuntium ad urbem mittere parat.
3. cur in silvas venire times, Marce?
4. scitisne cantare, pueri?
5. dux castra hostium oppugnare non timet.
6. socii auxilium mittere ad Romanos parant.
7. senex per forum errare et templa spectare amat.

8. servi sex mensas in triclinium movere parant.
9. in horto sub umbra arboris dormire amo.
10. scisne gladium tenere, Gai?

Other verbs which are often followed by an Infinitive include:

debeo	**(2)**	I ought to, must
constituo	**(3)**	I decide
nescio	**(4)**	I do not know (how)

EXERCISE 6.2

1. ad ludum festinare debetis, pueri.
2. frater ducis ad urbem revenire constituit.
3. puer regi respondere nescit.
4. matrem iuvare debes, Quinte.
5. ego cum comitibus in mari natare paro.
6. filius Marci miles esse constituit.
7. hodie servus agricolae in agris laborare non amat, quod sol est calidus.
8. Horatius pontem custodire constituit.
9. Mucius regem gladio necare parat.
10. Cloelia trans flumen natare non timet.

EXERCISE 6.3

1. I like to swim in the sea.
2. You ought not to run into the road, boys.
3. The consul decides to remain in the city.
4. The boy is afraid to run into the waves.
5. The farmers do not know how to fight with spears.

There are some verbs in both Latin and English which need an Infinitive **after their object**; these are usually verbs of **ordering etc.**

e.g.	**iubeo**	**(2)**	I order, tell
	veto	**(1)**	I forbid, tell not to
	cogo	**(3)**	I compel, force

EXERCISE 6.4

1. magister pueros laborare iubet.
2. pater filium dicere vetat.
3. dux milites per viam festinare cogit.
4. pueros in silvas errare veto.
5. mater pueros carmen novum audire iubet.
6. agricola servum in agris laborare cogit.
7. ad casam revenire ante noctem debetis.
8. Romulus cives mulieres Sabinas in urbem portare iubet.
9. mulieres patres viros oppugnare vetant.
10. feminae et patres et viros amicos esse cogunt.

EXERCISE 6.5

magister pueris in ludo dicit. pueri verba magistri audiunt, sed Marcus Publio subito dicit. magister et Marcum et Publium tacere iubet.

magister: tacete, pueri. scitisne fabulam de Coriolano?

Publius: fabulas antiquas de urbe Roma audire semper amo.

magister: Coriolanus est civis Romanus, sed, quod iratus est, ex urbe discedere constituit. ad castra hostium venit et contra patriam pugnare parat. deinde mulieres Romanae, quod pericula belli timent, ad matrem et uxorem Coriolani veniunt. mater uxorque verba mulierum audiunt. cum filiis parvis Coriolani ex urbe discedunt et ad castra hostium appropinquare parant.

Marcus: nonne feminae castra hostium intrare timent?

magister: et mater et uxor Coriolani feminae fortes sunt. castra hostium cum pueris intrant, et nuntius Coriolano dicit. Coriolanus ad matrem appropinquat, sed mater irata est. " esne hostis an filius?" inquit. Coriolanus respondet, "ego filius, non hostis, sum". itaque mater laeta est, et filium urbem Romam oppugnare vetat.

antiquus	ancient
discedo (3)	I leave, depart from
patria	own country/city
-que *	and
an	or
inquit	he/she says

*Note how this is attached to the end of the second word

e.g.   **pueri puellaeque**   boys <u>and</u> girls

EXERCISE 6.6

1.   You ought to be happy, Marcus.
2.   The schoolmaster orders the boys to listen to the story.
3.   The citizens decide to enter the ancient temple.
4.   The boys and girls are preparing to leave.
5.   The mother forbids her son to attack his own country.

EXERCISE 6.7

1.   Explain the meaning of the following English words, and show how they derive from Latin:

   alternate   celestial   interrogate   patriotic

2.   Find English derivations from the following Latin words, and write a sentence for each which clearly shows its meaning:

   constituo   dormio   invenio   occupo   verbum

THE ROMAN REPUBLIC

In Chapter 2 of Book 1 you were given a brief outline of Roman history. In this book we have been talking about legends which supposedly took place in the very early years of Rome's history.

It may be useful to remind you of some key dates from Rome's history, as given at the beginning of Book 1.

753 BC	Legendary founding of Rome
	Rome ruled by Kings until
509 BC	Rome is now a Republic
by 250 BC	Rome has control of central and southern Italy
by 100 BC	Rome has control of the Mediterranean area
44 BC	Murder of Julius Caesar
27 BC	Julius Caesar's adopted son becomes the first Emperor, taking the name Augustus.
	The Roman Empire in the west survives until
AD 476	Last Emperor of Rome is deposed by Germanic tribes
	The Eastern Roman Empire Lasts until:
AD 1453	Fall of Constantinople

You can see from the list above that the Roman kings ruled for nearly 250 years, but that the Roman republic lasted for almost twice as long.

When **Tarquin the Proud** was expelled, the Romans wanted a system which would not allow one man to gain too much power. They therefore elected two **consuls** each year, and for one year only. This was designed to prevent one of them from gaining excessive power.

They also had several other officers to assist in the running of the government, which was called the **senate** (from the word **senex** "an old man" – so that it was originally a Council of Elders).

These included **tribunes**, whose job it was especially to look after the interests of the ordinary people. At first there were only two of them, but soon afterwards there were ten each year, and they not only preserved the rights of the people, but could also summon assemblies, propose laws, stop the deliberations of the senate and even veto its decrees.

The nasty word during the Republican times was **"rex"** – this conjured up to a Roman the evil power that we might associate with **Hitler** or **Stalin**. Our word **"dictator"** was in fact first used by the Romans during the Republic, and this title was given to a man in an emergency when it was felt that the consuls could not cope. In normal times the office of dictator was held for only six months.

This system lasted well for the Romans for several centuries, but by around **100BC** Rome had become a dominant power, vastly changed from the small city state for which the Republic had been set up four centuries earlier. Rome was in fact now an empire, and her empire grew over the next fifty years. What Rome needed was an emperor. Julius Caesar tried in effect to become one. He was not the first to abuse the office of **"dictator"**, but the Roman nobles feared that he was – even worse – trying to become a **"rex"**! They therefore formed the plot to kill him on the **Ides of March in 44BC**.

Civil War followed his death between his trusted supporter, **Mark Antony**, and his adopted son, **Octavian**. It was Octavian who at last won the war at the **Battle of Actium in 31BC**, and four years later he became Rome's first emperor, taking the title **Augustus**.

EXERCISE 6.8

1. From the dates given above write a date chart in your own books.

2. You may by now have discovered that Shakespeare wrote plays about Julius Caesar and about Antony & Cleopatra. Choose one of these and find out more about the plot of the play.

3. Why do imagine people like Julius Caesar or Hitler want to gain so much power? Do you think that it is inevitable that there will be dictators trying to abuse power? Can you think of anybody like this in the world today?

PERSONAL PRONOUNS

7

You have already met the Latin words for "I" (**ego**), "we" (**nos**) "you" (**tu** and **vos**). These are the Subject pronouns in the **Nominative Case**.

Here below are **all the cases** of these pronouns.

NOM	ego	nōs		tū	vōs
VOC	–	–		tū	vōs
ACC	mē	nōs		tē	vōs
GEN	meī	nostrī/nostrum		tuī	vestrī/vestrum
DAT	mihi	nōbīs		tibi	vōbīs
ABL	mē	nōbīs		tē	vōbīs

These pronouns are used in the different cases just like nouns:

e.g.　　　pater **me** videt
　　　　　Father sees **me**

　　　　　mater librum **mihi** dat
　　　　　Mother gives the book **to me**

EXERCISE 7.1

1.　pater te in urbem mittit.
2.　pater materque nos in atrio exspectant.
3.　cur agricola pecuniam vobis dat?
4.　miles me hasta non terret.
5.　ego tibi librum novum monstro.
6.　cur tu ad me epistolam non mittis, Iulia?
7.　mene audis, Marce?
8.　nonne magister te laudat, Gai?
9.　socii auxilium a nobis exspectant.
10.　vos in viam currere veto.

EXERCISE 7.2

1. The poet is calling you into the garden.
2. Mother is telling us a new story.
3. Many soldiers are fighting against us.
4. Why aren't you helping me, Marcus?
5. I am sending five slaves to you today.

These pronouns can also be used **reflexively** to mean **"myself, "yourself"** etc.:

e.g   **me** curo
         I look after **myself**

         cur **vos** vulneratis?
         Why are you wounding **yourselves**?

There is also a **Third Person Reflexive Pronoun** (**se**) which can be either **Singular or Plural** and mean **"himself, herself, itself or themselves"**.

It declines like this:

ACC	sē
GEN	suī
DAT	sibi
ABL	sē

EXERCISE 7.3

1. puer se in aqua fluminis videt.
2. Iulia cibum sibi in culina parat.
3. cur te non curas, senex?
4. rex malus se laudat.
5. milites ad bellum se parant.
6. servus in silva se celat.
7. me a periculo servare constituo.
8. te iuvare debes, Marce.
9. nos ad pericula belli paramus.
10. cur te in mare iacis, Gai?

If **cum** is used with any of these pronouns, it is attached to the end of them:

e.g.   **mēcum**   with me

            nōbiscum   with us

EXERCISE 7.4

1. nonne tu mecum ad urbem venis, Marce?
2. multi iuvenes nobiscum in horto ambulant.
3. puer libros tabulasque secum ad ludum portat.
4. magister nobis aliam fabulam hodie narrat.
5. tune nobiscum ad insulam navigas, Tullia?
6. cur tu ante me stas, Quinte?
7. agricola et cibum et vinum sibi parat.
8. decem servi nobiscum in villa habitant.
9. nonne tu mecum ad theatrum venis, Gai?
10. quis tecum ad forum ambulat, Iulia?

EXERCISE 7.5

1. Father is sending you to the city.
2. Who is calling us into the garden?
3. We are sailing with you across the river.
4. The leader is preparing himself before the battle.
5. The girls are giving us both wine and flowers.

EXERCISE 7.6

milites Romani in ponte stant. hostes appropinquant. Horatius clamat.

Horatius: hostes urbem Romam occupare parant. ad pontem currunt. itaque pontem delere debemus. comites, vos curate et ad urbem festinate.

milites: a ponte sine te discedere non amamus.

Horatius milites discedere iubet, sed duo comites, nomine Spurius et Titus, manere constituunt. tandem Horatius iterum clamat.

Horatius: delete pontem <u>statim</u>. nunc vos quoque discedere debetis.

Spurius: nonne tu nobiscum venis?

Horatius: ego in ponte sto et patriam ab hostibus servo. deos auxilium oro.

Titus: te serva, Horati.

duo comites a ponte discedunt et ad alteram ripam reveniunt. Horatius caelum spectat.

Horatius: <u>di</u>, me iuvate et urbem Romam servate.

deinde Horatius cum gladio armisque in aquas fluminis se iacit. hostes tela iaciunt, sed Horatius per tela et alia pericula ad alteram ripam natat. comites laeti virum salutant.

statim	at once, immediately
di	Nom and Voc Plural of **deus**

EXERCISE 7.7

1. Two companions are waiting with me.
2. Surely the gods are helping you?
3. The enemy decide to destroy the city at once.
4. The soldiers are now running through the enemies' weapons.
5. I find a large sword in the river.

LATIN LITERATURE

The stories that have been told so far in this book are all part of Rome's early history, written by **Livy** who lived in the reign of the first emperor **Augustus**, (see last chapter).

Augustus did not want to die at the hands of assassins, just as **Julius Caesar** had done, and he needed the support of the nobility – what we today might call the "chattering classes".

He therefore encouraged writers who through their **literature** would spread **patriotism** and in particular support for the new regime. This could be done as much by looking at the great deeds of the past as by glorifying the emperor's current achievements – which incidentally he did in a small work of his own, recorded on stone!

History was just one type of literature favoured by the new emperor. He also wanted **poetry** to record the glory of Rome. Two poets in particular were loyal to his ideals and wrote poetry of very different kinds to support Augustus' new regime.

One of these poets was **Virgil**. He wrote the **Georgics**, a poem about farming which was mentioned in the final chapter of Book 1. However, his most famous poem is called the **Aeneid**. This is an epic poem in twelve books which describes the wanderings of Aeneas after the sack of Troy.

Aeneas first travels to Carthage where he meets the beautiful queen **Dido**, who falls desperately in love with him. It is not, however, part of the divine plan for Aeneas to remain in Africa, and **Jupiter** sends **Mercury**, the messenger god, to remind Aeneas of his duty. Aeneas unhesitatingly obeys and continues his journey to **Italy**, where he has to fight the local inhabitants before he can establish a new city for himself and his followers.

Many see the **Aeneid** as having a message for Virgil's readers. They were living in a new age brought in by the emperor Augustus, and the old tales of Aeneas' troubles to found a new city are meant to reflect the emperor's attempts to rebuild Rome after the civil wars which he had now ended. There are also passages in this long poem where Virgil clearly shows his approval of Augustus – this is what is called **political propaganda**.

So literature, both epic poetry and history, was being used to persuade the readers of their past glories and to take a pride in their city, which Augustus was busily rebuilding. It was in fact the emperor's boast that he had found the city in brick and left it in marble!

The third famous writer of Augustus' reign is the poet **Horace**. He wrote a wide variety of poetry, but much of it clearly praises the new regime and talks of the blessings that Augustus has brought to the Roman people.

EXERCISE 7.8

1. Find out more about the stories in the Aeneid. Ask your teacher to tell you some, and/or go to the library to see if you can learn more there.

2. Why do you think Augustus needed literature to support him? Do you know of other rulers who have tried to use writers in this way?

3. As was said above, this type of literature is called "propaganda". Do you know of other types of propaganda that have been used in this century for political ends?

4. Do you think that advertising is propaganda?

MORE ADJECTIVES 8

In Chapter 15 of Book 1 you learnt about adjectives.

You have now learnt Neuter nouns as well and so here below is the full declension of **magnus** including the **Neuter** endings, which you will see are those of **vinum** just as the **Masculine** are those of **servus** and the **Feminine** those of **puella**.

These adjectives are therefore called **1st/2nd Declension**.

SINGULAR

	MASCULINE	FEMININE	NEUTER
NOM	magn**us**	magn**a**	magn**um**
VOC	magn**e**	magn**a**	magn**um**
ACC	magn**um**	magn**am**	magn**um**
GEN	magn**ī**	magn**ae**	magn**ī**
DAT	magn**ō**	magn**ae**	magn**ō**
ABL	magn**ō**	magn**ā**	magn**ō**

PLURAL

	MASCULINE	FEMININE	NEUTER
NOM	magn**ī**	magn**ae**	magn**a**
VOC	magn**ī**	magn**ae**	magn**a**
ACC	magn**ōs**	magn**ās**	magn**a**
GEN	magn**ōrum**	magn**ārum**	magn**ōrum**
DAT	magn**īs**	magn**īs**	magn**īs**
ABL	magn**īs**	magn**īs**	magn**īs**

Sometimes the noun and adjective have the same ending:

e.g   cas**a** pulchr**a**   a beautiful house

But not always:

e.g   mult**i** civ**es**   many citizens

This depends on the **group (or declension)** of the noun and adjective, but **REMEMBER** that the noun and adjective **ALWAYS** agree in these **THREE WAYS**:

> 1) **Number** – Singular or Plural
> 2) **Gender** – Masculine or Feminine
> 3) **Case** – Nominative, Accusative etc.

Here are some more adjectives like **magnus** to learn before doing the next exercises:

longus	long
notus	well-known
saevus	fierce, savage
solus	alone
tutus	safe
validus	strong

If an adjective is used with an infinitive, then it always has a **Neuter** ending.

e.g.   bon**um** est ambulare
             It is good to walk

EXERCISE 8.1

1. pueri fabulas longas audire amant.
2. casa poetae est nota multis civibus.
3. saevi hostes senes hastis longis terrent.
4. tu in silvis solus ambulare non debes, Marce.
5. non semper tutum est in mari alto ludere.
6. dux hostium oppidum validum oppugnare parat.
7. regina pulchra iuvenem in Africa secum tenet.
8. vir fortis in ponte solus manere non timet.

9. num tutum est puellis trans flumen natare?
10. mulieres castra hostium saevorum intrare non timent.

EXERCISE 8.2

Rewrite the following sentences, putting the nouns, verbs and adjectives into the plural, and then translate them into English.

1. civis canem saevum timet.
2. dux oppidum validum occupat.
3. mulier fessa carmen longum non audit.
4. equus ducis tutus est in magno agro.
5. magnus puer florem pulchrum puellae parvae dat.

There are also adjectives which have endings of the **3rd Declension**. Most of these have the extra **-i-** of nouns like **mare** (see page 29)

So the   **ABL SING**   ends in   **-ī**
          GEN PLUR   ends in   **-ium**
          NOM/ACC NEUTER PLUR   end in   **-ia**

fortis (brave) which you have now met in several exercises is an example of this kind of adjective, and its full declension is as follows and should now be learnt:

	SINGULAR		PLURAL	
	MASC/FEM	NEUTER	MASC/FEM	NEUTER
NOM/VOC	fortis	forte	fortēs	fortia
ACC	fortem	forte	fortēs	fortia
GEN	fortis	fortis	fortium	fortium
DAT	fortī	fortī	fortibus	fortibus
ABL	fortī	fortī	fortibus	fortibus

Other adjectives like this include:

brevis   short
crudelis   cruel
difficilis   difficult
dulcis   sweet

facilis	easy
gravis	heavy, serious
omnis	every
qualis?	what sort of?
tristis	sad

EXERCISE 8.3

1. milites fortes per viam difficilem festinant.
2. verba crudelia magistri pueros terrent.
3. non facile est trans montes ambulare.
4. omnes cives consulem in foro exspectant.
5. quales mensas habes, serve? num graves sunt?
6. difficile est nobis ad oram ante noctem revenire.
7. senex festinare constituit, quod via est brevis et facilis.
8. dux servos vinum dulce omnibus comitibus dare iubet.
9. rex crudelis iuvenes ex urbe discedere vetat.
10. puer tristis est, quod corpus canis in via invenit.

EXERCISE 8.4

1. All the slaves are carrying the heavy table.
2. The cruel leader frightens the wretched citizens.
3. It is difficult to remain on the bridge.
4. What sort of soldiers are there in the camp?
5. The brave boy kills the savage dog with a large stone.

There are some other 3rd Declension adjectives such as **audax** (bold, daring) which have the same ending for **MASC, FEM & NEUTER NOM SING and NEUTER ACC SING**; thereafter their endings are the same as for **fortis**, as you can see from the table below.

	SINGULAR		PLURAL	
	MASC/FEM	**NEUTER**	**MASC/FEM**	**NEUTER**
NOM/VOC	auda**x**	auda**x**	audac**ēs**	audac**ia**
ACC	audac**em**	auda**x**	audac**ēs**	audac**ia**
GEN	audac**is**	audac**is**	audac**ium**	audac**ium**
DAT	audac**ī**	audac**ī**	audac**ibus**	audac**ibus**
ABL	audac**ī**	audac**ī**	audac**ibus**	audac**ibus**

These adjectives you need to learn with their genitive, in order to know the stem.

e.g. **audax, audacis**

Others like this include:

felix, felicis	happy, lucky
ferox, ferocis	fierce
ingens, ingentis	huge
sapiens, sapientis	wise

EXERCISE 8.5

1. filius regis est iuvenis audax.
2. difficile est animal ingens necare.
3. taurus agricolae est ferox et saevus.
4. bonum est pueros felices spectare.
5. comites audaces in silvas currere parant.
6. pater sapiens pueros in via ludere vetat.
7. qualis vir est dux militum? nonne est audax est fortis?
8. felices estis, pueri, quod magister in ludum hodie non venit.
9. servi consulis villam ingentem prope flumen altum aedificant.
10. vir audax pontem delet et in flumen cadit.

EXERCISE 8.6

DIDO AND AENEAS

Graeci Troiam occupant. itaque Aeneas cum patre et filio et aliis comitibus ab urbe discedit. ad Italiam navigant, sed dea Iuno tempestatem ingentem mittit et multas naves delet.

Aeneas cum <u>paucis</u> comitibus ad Africam venit. ad urbem appropinquant et regina urbis, nomine Dido, iuvenem <u>valde</u> amat. regina est femina pulchra et Aeneas in Africa manere amat.

Iuppiter, <u>tamen</u>, iratus est et Mercurium, nuntium deorum, ad iuvenem mittit. nuntius iuvenem miserum in Africa manere vetat et statim discedere iubet. Aeneas deis paret, sed regina <u>valde</u> tristis est et se necare parat.

pauci	a few
valde	very (much)
tamen	however

EXERCISE 8.7

responde Latine:

1. cur Aeneas cum comitibus ab urbe Troia discedit?
2. quis tempestatem ingentem mittit?
3. qualis femina est regina?
4. ubi Aeneas manere amat?
5. cur regina est valde tristis?

EXERCISE 8.8

1. The huge storm destroys the ships.
2. A few companions remain in the city.
3. The beautiful queen greets the messenger.
4. The gods order the young man to leave at once.
5. Surely the sad queen does not kill herself?

EXERCISE 8.9

1. Explain the meaning of the following English words, and show how they derive from Latin:

    audacious   facilitate   notoriety   solitude

2. Find English derivations from the following Latin words, and write a sentence for each which clearly shows its meaning:

    ferox   fortis   gravis   magnus

PLAYS

Another type of literature is **drama**, which concerns **plays**. We have been referring to plays written by our own **William Shakespeare**. Plays in the ancient world date back to an age much earlier than that of the **emperor Augustus**. It is perhaps interesting to note that the Latin word **fabula** means not only "a story" (as you know), but also "a play".

Roman plays were adapted from Greek models, both **tragedy** and **comedy**. However, the Romans far preferred comedy. The two famous Latin comic playwrights were in fact not Roman at all. **Plautus** came from an Italian country town, while **Terence** was originally an African who had come to Rome as a slave.

Plautus was the elder of these two, and wrote his plays around 200BC. **Terence** was writing about forty years later. Their comedies were very much based on Greek plays known as New Comedy. Another ingredient for their humour came from popular farces, which also contained **"stock" characters**, such as an old man, a greedy ogre and two fools.

Plautus' plays were very much based on the lower end of Roman society, and continued to be popular throughout the Roman era. There was often an irresponsible young man who was hopelessly in love and in debt, with a strict father and a resourceful slave. The plots were very much like our farces, and always had a happy ending.

Terence kept more closely to the Greek plays which he was imitating, and his plays were rather more sophisticated than those of Plautus. Perhaps for this reason his plays were less popular, but he believed, like his Greek predecessors, that it was his duty not merely to entertain his audience, but also to instruct them. Certainly his ideas did have an influence on later European writers.

Costumes denoted the various characters: for instance, the rich wore purple, and prostitutes yellow. The basic garment was a tunic, pulled over the head and tied with a girdle. Often they wore a woollen cloak as well, and sometimes a hat, especially if they were travellers.

The actors also wore **masks,** to denote what sort of character they were. This practice also comes from the Greek theatre, and one ancient writer lists no less than 44 different types of comic mask!

Other types of theatrical performance included **mime** and **pantomime**. **Mime** was usually presented by a single actor, accompanied by pipes. Mime actors did not wear masks, but relied on facial distortion and exaggerated gestures.

Pantomime developed from mime and was a popular form of entertainment at the time of Augustus. Most pantomime dancers were men, and often gave a solo performance, playing many different parts, changing their masks to do so. They had to be clever and imaginative as well as physically strong and well trained. Several instruments might accompany their shows, and the subject matter might be about an epic or tragic story.

Acting had been considered a respectable profession in Greece, and in Athens the winning actor became something of a national hero – a little like the stars of the modern era.

In Rome, however, the position of **actors** was very different. Many of them were foreigners, slaves or freedmen, and they were therefore despised. Indeed a company of actors was known as a **"grex"** – meaning "herd" or "flock". Actors could even be whipped for gross behaviour during a performance, and actresses were thought of as being no better than prostitutes. The **emperor Tiberius**, who succeeded Augustus, went as far as to expel actors from Italy because of their supposedly immoral behaviour.

Yet, although the majority of **actors** led poor and obscure lives, the rewards of success for some could be very high. Some earned fame and fortune, and slave actors sometimes gained their freedom by the quality of their performance. The successful actor would be welcomed in society, especially if he/she was good-looking, and the **emperor Nero** enjoyed appearing on the public stage both as actor and musician. When he died (at his own hand), his last words were said to be **"qualis artifex pereo"** – "what an artist dies in me!!"

EXERCISE 8.10

1. Find from your school or local library a translation of a play by Plautus or Terence and read it round the class.

2. Draw pictures of how you think Roman actors would have looked in costume.

3. What makes <u>you</u> laugh? Do you think that humour changes much over the centuries?

ADVERBS

9

Adverbs are words which go with verbs and describe **how, when or where** the action of the verb takes place.

e.g.　　　We run **quickly**
　　　　　We will arrive **soon**

Among the adverbs you have already learnt are :

hodie	today
iterum	again
mox	soon
nunc	now
saepe	often
semper	always
subito	suddenly
statim	at once
tandem	at last
valde	very much

EXERCISE 9.1

1.　hodie ad urbem revenimus.
2.　magister puerum malum e ludo iterum mittit.
3.　nunc est nuntius consulis in atrio.
4.　fabulas de viris fortibus saepe auditis.
5.　pueri magistris semper parere debent.
6.　subito iuvenis in mare se iacit.
7.　hostes urbem statim oppugnare constituunt.
8.　tandem servi cenam in mensam ponunt.
9.　regina iuvenem fortem valde amat.
10.　deus oculos ducis somno mox superat.

As in English, so in Latin adverbs are often formed from adjectives.

e.g.
bene	well
laete	happily
longe	far
pulchre	beautifully
audacter	boldly
crudeliter	cruelly
ferociter	fiercely
fortiter	bravely
sapienter	wisely

and many more including:

lente	slowly
celeriter	quickly

EXERCISE 9.2

1. pueri et puellae prope flumen laete sedent.
2. rex feminas puerosque ex urbe crudeliter mittit.
3. filia poetae pulchre cantat.
4. per viam longam lente ambulare constituo.
5. milites contra hostes fortiter pugnant.
6. puer e casa in hortum celeriter currit.
7. senex longe ab urbe habitat.
8. iuvenis castra hostium audacter intrat.
9. dux comites de periculis belli bene monet.
10. magister pueros sapienter docet.

EXERCISE 9.3

1. The boys are running quickly towards the ships.
2. The girl often gives flowers to her mother.
3. The guards bravely enter the camp.
4. Suddenly we hear the fierce voice of the leader.
5. The old man walks slowly with me into the field.

You have now often met the **Imperative** of verbs for giving orders. This is a good time to learn/revise the **Imperative endings of all four groups**, and of **sum**.

Singular	amā	vidē	rege	audī	es/estō
Plural	amāte	vidēte	regite	audīte	este

Note how rego changes its vowel!

EXERCISE 9.4

1. ambula lente per viam, Tullia.
2. regite urbem sapienter, consules.
3. pugnate fortiter, milites.
4. dormi bene, Iulia.
5. semper este boni et parete patri, pueri.
6. venite mecum ad forum hodie, amici.
7. ponite vinum in mensam statim, servi.
8. discedite ex urbe ante noctem, comites.
9. iube cives consuli audacter respondere.
10. narra nobis iterum fabulam de regina pulchra, pater.

EXERCISE 9.5

1. Run quickly into the house, friends.
2. Always lie down in the shade, Marcus.
3. Be bold, girls, and reply to the queen.
4. Come at once into the atrium, Quintus.
5. Teach the boys wisely, schoolmaster.

EXERCISE 9.6

AENEAS ARRIVES IN ITALY

Aeneas naves celeriter parat et ex Africa cum comitibus discedit. Dido se necat, sed dux Troianorum nescit. in <u>itinere</u> sunt multae tempestates, multi venti, multa pericula, sed Troiani ad Italiam tandem <u>adveniunt</u>. omnes sunt fessi et miseri.

Aeneas urbem novam sibi et suis comitibus aedificare parat. incolae tamen non laeti sunt. multi incolae ad bellum arma parant, et contra Troianos in proelio pugnant. subito rex incolarum, nomine Latinus, ducem Troianorum ad se vocat. rex ducem salutat et "quis es?" rogat. "quomodo ad Italiam advenis?" "ego sum Aeneas, dux Troianorum et filius deae Veneris," respondet Aeneas. " post multa pericula ad Italiam advenio." duo viri de pace et de bello diu dicunt. tandem rex pacem habere constituit et filiam quoque iuveni ad matrimonium dat.

iter, itineris (n)	journey
advenio (4)	I arrive
quomodo?	how?
diu	for a long time
matrimonium, ii (n)	marriage

EXERCISE 9.7

responde Latine:

1. quomodo Aeneas naves parat?
2. ubi sunt multae tempestates?
3. cur incolae non laeti sunt?
4. quis ducem salutat?
5. quis est Aeneas?

EXERCISE 9.8

1. The sad queen quickly kills herself.
2. We arrive at last after many storms.
3. All the inhabitants are preparing their weapons.
4. The leader decides to wait on the ship for a long time.
5. The young man happily replies to the beautiful girl.

THEATRES

The plays written by **Plautus** and **Terence**, which you read about in the last chapter, were put on in theatres which were rather different from those of today.

The **Greeks** had built splendid theatres, such as the one which survives at **Epidauros** today. Some of you may have seen this wonderful theatre, and even have seen a play there.

It is a large open-air theatre, very much larger than any modern theatre, and could hold up to 20,000 spectators. The circular space at the bottom is called the **orchestra**, which is where people danced and sang. Behind is the **stage** itself and the stage buildings.

At the time of **Plautus** there was no permanent theatre in Rome. The Greeks had built some of their splendid theatres (like the one at Epidauros) elsewhere in Italy and Sicily, but the Romans had not yet imitated them. Instead temporary wooden buildings were constructed for the performances.

Plautus needed for his plays a long wooden stage, which represented a street, and a building behind the stage which normally showed the fronts of houses. All the action took place outside in the street, and there was little scenery.

Pompey, who lived at the same time as **Julius Caesar**, built the first permanent stone theatre in Rome – but it does not survive. One of the reasons that theatres were not at first built in Rome may have been because they were thought to damage the morality of the people! However, **Augustus** built two new theatres in Rome, one of which was dedicated to his **nephew Marcellus** after he died young, and part of this you can see in Rome today.

Theatre at Orange

Roman theatres did not have **curtains** as we do today in most theatres. A curtain was used, but it was only a few metres high, and was fixed in a slot at the front of the stage. At the start of the play it was taken down, and then raised at the end of the play.

There were three separate tiers of seats in the theatres, with segregation according to class – and sex! The **audience** had to sit for many hours on these stone seats and under a hot sun – imagine how uncomfortable this would be! You may have experienced this, if you have visited a stone theatre such as the one at **Bradfield College**.

There were, however, some **comforts** provided. Canvas covers gave protection from the sun, and some people would bring parasols with them. As today in a stone theatre the audience might take cushions to sit on. Sometimes the seats were sprinkled with a plant like saffron – to offset the smell of body sweat!! Also like today, food and drinks were provided, but very often the spectators brought their own "picnic" with them. The audiences behaved more rowdily than in modern theatres, and if they did not like the play they would show it – by booing, hissing or even walking out!

EXERCISE 9.9

1. Write out a list of as many differences you can think of between the ancient and the modern theatre.

2. Having now, I hope, read a play by Plautus or Terence, why not try to produce a scene or two – using the classroom or, if you are allowed, your school stage?

3. Draw a plan or even make a model of a Greek or Roman theatre.

THE IMPERFECT TENSE

10

So far the only tense that you have met in these books is the **Present** – i.e. referring to what is happening now. This has also been used in stories about the past, as Roman writers commonly used the Present in this way, as we often do, and you should have had no difficulty in translating it.

The **Imperfect** is the name given to a tense in Latin which describes a **repeated, continuous or interrrupted action which took place in the past.**

e.g.   **I used to swim** every morning.
         I was working when the telephone rang.

Both of the highlighted tenses are **Imperfect** – which in fact means incomplete. The action took place in the past, but it was unfinished.

The endings of the tense are as follows:

-bam	I
-bās	you
-bat	he, she, it
-bāmus	we
-bātis	you (pl)
-bant	they

You will note that the final endings correspond to those you learnt for the Present tense in Chapter 8 of Book 1 with an extra **ba-** added. The final **-m** for "I" is like that at the end of **su<u>m</u>** "I am".

So   **I used to swim** is in Latin   **natabam**
         I was working is   **laborabam**

This tense can be translated by **"was doing"** or **"used to do"** or sometimes **"began to do"** and you need to choose the best meaning according to what makes most sense.

These endings are attached directly to the verb stem of the first and second groups of verbs, but the the **third and fourth add an extra -e** as shown below:

ama**bam**	vide**bam**	rege**bam**	audie**bam**
ama**bās**	vide**bās**	rege**bās**	audie**bās**
ama**bat**	vide**bat**	rege**bat**	audie**bat**
ama**bāmus**	vide**bāmus**	rege**bāmus**	audie**bāmus**
ama**bātis**	vide**bātis**	rege**bātis**	audie**bātis**
ama**bant**	vide**bant**	rege**bant**	audie**bant**

EXERCISE 10.1

1. mittebamus.
2. dormiebat.
3. sedebam.
4. errabatis.
5. iuvabamus.
6. docebam.
7. dicebas.
8. ponebant.
9. veniebat.
10. laudabatis.

EXERCISE 10.2

1. I was walking.
2. He was falling.
3. You (sing) used to swim.
4. We used to sing.
5. They were sitting.
6. We were sailing.
7. She was arriving.
8. You (plur) were shouting.
9. I used to sail.
10. He began to fight.

EXERCISE 10.3

1.   in theatrum celeriter currebamus.
2.   saepe in flumine cum sorore natabam.
3.   mater fabulas mihi semper narrabat.
4.   novem servi lectum gravem portabant.
5.   ego te de periculis itineris saepe monebam.
6.   cur tu verba magistri non audiebas, male puer?
7.   rex urbem bene et sapienter regebat.
8.   ad oram insulae ante noctem adveniebamus.
9.   lux lunae viam nobis monstrabat.
10. puer de arbore saepe cadebat.

EXERCISE 10.4

1.   tres puellae nobiscum in ripa sedebant.
2.   magistro audacter respondebam.
3.   libertus quinque mensas in hortum movebat.
4.   animal ferox me non terrebat.
5.   in urbe cum fratre diu manebam.
6.   magister pueros tacere iubebat.
7.   multas fabulas in theatro spectabamus.
8.   cur tu ad me epistolas non mittebas, Iulia?
9.   incolae multa arma ad proelium parabant.
10. mater dolebat, quod filius post bellum non reveniebat.

EXERCISE 10.5

1.   The slaves were working in the farmer's fields.
2.   We were watching the beautiful girls in the theatre.
3.   Why were you sleeping before dinner, Marcus?
4.   The messenger was putting six letters on to the table.
5.   We often used to see large animals in the woods.

The **Imperfect tense** of the verb **sum** is as follows:

> **eram**
> **erās**
> **erat**
> **erāmus**
> **erātis**
> **erant**

This can be translated as **"I was/used to be"**

EXERCISE 10.6

1. Aeneas erat dux Troianorum.
2. servi erant fessi, quod diu laborabant.
3. cur in urbe sine matre eras, Iulia?
4. quis erat dux hostium?
5. in agro erant multi tauri.
6. in magno periculo eramus.
7. num in silvis eratis, pueri?
8. nonne vinum erat dulce?
9. regina tristis erat, quod nautae discedere parabant.
10. Horatius fortis erat, quod in ponte contra hostes solus stabat.

EXERCISE 10.7

Write out Exercise 1.1 but put each of the verbs into the **Imperfect** tense, and then translate into English.

Before translating the next exercises learn these new verbs from the **Third Conjugation**:

ascendo	I climb
descendo	I go down
duco	I lead, take
lego	I read
ludo	I play
peto	I look for, seek, ask for
trado	I hand over
vinco	I defeat, conquer

EXERCISE 10.8

1. fabulas antiquas saepe legebamus.
2. pueri in horto laete ludebant.
3. agricola gregem longe ab oppido ducebat.
4. nautae miseri cibum prope oram petebant.
5. montem ingentem audacter ascendebatis.
6. senex pecuniam filio tradere parabat.
7. hostes celeriter vincere debetis.
8. descende lente de arbore, Marce.
9. puer alium librum legere sapienter constituebat.
10. rex filiam pulchram iuveni ad matrimonium tradebat.

EXERCISE 10.9

1. We often used to play in the garden.
2. I was taking my son to the theatre.
3. The old man was looking for his daughter in the forum.
4. Climb the mountain with us, Quintus.
5. You ought to read the book again.

EXERCISE 10.10

1. Explain the meaning of the following English words, and show how they derive from Latin:

    gregarious   itinerary   petition   tradition

2. Find English derivations from the following Latin words, and write a sentence for each which clearly shows its meaning:

    descendo   ludo   matrimonium   mitto

AMPHITHEATRES

In the last chapter you read about theatre buildings. Another kind of building used for entertainment in the Roman world was the **amphitheatre**. This long word in fact means "double theatre", and amphitheatres were oval shaped.

The stadium consisted of an arena covered in sand (**arena** is the Latin word for "sand") and was surrounded – as in the theatre – by banked tiers of seats with the same separations for different types of people. The best seats were reserved for the emperor and his family in the **Imperial Box**, which was fitted with a secret underground passageway – in case of emergencies!

The earliest surviving amphitheatre is that at **Pompeii** in southern Italy, which was built around 70BC. In Rome before **Augustus** temporary enclosures had been used for shows, but it was Augustus who built the first stone amphitheatre in Rome.

The most famous amphitheatre in the Roman world is the **Colosseum** in the centre of Rome. This building was built by the emperor **Vespasian** who founded the new **Flavian** dynasty of emperors. It was dedicated by his son **Titus** in AD80 with a lavish display of games which went on for one hundred days. It was in fact then known as the **Amphitheatrum Flavium** (Flavian Amphitheatre). The name Colosseum has nothing to do with the size of this building, but comes from the huge statue – or **Colossus** – of the **emperor Nero** which stood nearby.

The **Colosseum** held up to 50,000 spectators, of whom all but 5,000 could be seated. There were eighty entrance arches, of which thirty still survive, and this number of entrances limited the chance of any crush at the start or end of the shows.

The types of shows which were performed will be described in the next chapters. Today some amphitheatres are still used, but for very different purposes – such as the one at **Nîmes** in France for bull-fighting or the one at **Verona** in northern Italy for opera.

Occasionally the amphitheatres were flooded in order to stage mock sea-battles, but modern engineers are hard pressed to work out exactly how so much water was brought into the arena, and then emptied again!

Amphitheatres were built all over the Roman empire, and remains of some can be seen in parts of Britain, such as at **Caerleon** in Wales or **Chester** in northern England.

If you visit Rome, the Colosseum is one of the main tourist attractions, but it is a mere shadow of its former self: the arena has lost its surface and there is hardly a trace of the marble seats. It is not easy to recapture the sights, the sounds and the stench of the bloodthirsty games that regularly took place there, but, with the throng of noisy tourists from all over the world, you can perhaps imagine the clamour and excitement that would have been among the crowds of nearly two millennia ago!!

EXERCISE 10.11

1. Compare the seating arrangements in the Colosseum with that of a modern football stadium.

2. Why do you think that emperors were keen to build amphitheatres in different parts of the Roman empire?

THE FUTURE TENSE

11

Here is another tense for you to learn!

Below are the endings of the Future tense for 1st and 2nd Conjugation Verbs:

ama**bō**	vide**bo**
ama**bis**	vide**bis**
ama**bit**	vide**bit**
ama**bimus**	vide**bimus**
ama**bitis**	vide**bitis**
ama**bunt**	vide**bunt**

The **Future** tense in Latin corresponds to the Future in English, i.e. **"will/shall"**.

So   **amabunt**   means   **they will love**

          videbo   means   **I shall see**

You will notice that the endings are quite similar to those of the Imperfect tense. It might be helpful to remember that the **a** of **-b<u>a</u>t** corresponds with the **a** of "w**as**", while the **i** of **-b<u>i</u>t** corresponds with the **i** of **w<u>i</u>ll**.

Note too that whereas there is an **a** all the way through the **Imperfect**, in the Future the **i** disappears before **-o** in **-bo** in the 1st person singular and becomes a **u** in **-bunt** in the 3rd person plural.

EXERCISE 11.1

1. aedificabimus.
2. cantabis.
3. monebo.

4. docebit.
5. manebunt.
6. dabo.
7. laudabit.
8. non timebo.
9. nonne iuvabis?
10. num dolebitis?

EXERCISE 11.2

1. He will walk.
2. They will sail.
3. We shall reply.
4. She will sit.
5. I will greet.
6. They will kill.
7. We will call.
8. I will not weep.
9. Surely we will not be afraid?
10. Surely you will work, Marcus?

EXERCISE 11.3

1. villam novam prope flumen aedificabo.
2. filiumne de periculis urbis monebis?
3. filia poetae ante cenam cantabit.
4. magister pueros bonos laudabit.
5. rex nautas de itinere rogabit.
6. servi aliam mensam in triclinium movebunt.
7. num duci respondebis, Gai?
8. nonne tacebitis, pueri mali?
9. vos statim discedere iubebo.
10. pater te in amphitheatro diu manere vetabit.

EXERCISE 11.4

Write out Exercise 3.1 but put each of the verbs into the **Future** tense, and then translate into English.

EXERCISE 11.5

1. The old men will hide the money under the tree.
2. We shall not wander into the woods.
3. Surely the enemy will not destroy the houses?
4. I will see you in the forum before night.
5. The wise schoolmaster will teach the boys well.

The endings of the **Future tense** are quite different for verbs of
the **3rd and 4th Conjugations**, and need to be carefully learnt.

reg**am**	audi**am**
reg**ēs**	audi**ēs**
reg**et**	audi**et**
reg**ēmus**	audi**ēmus**
reg**ētis**	audi**ētis**
reg**ent**	audi**ent**

So   **reget**   means   **he will rule**

        audiemus   means   **we shall listen**

EXERCISE 11.6

1. ascendemus.
2. mittam.
3. veniet.
4. scietis.
5. cades.
6. petam.
7. bene dormietis.
8. sapienter reget.
9. num curres?
10. quomodo discedemus?

EXERCISE 11.7

1. I shall speak.
2. We will play.
3. They will conquer.
4. He will rule.
5. She will find.

6. We will go down.
7. They will not come.
8. Who will lead?
9. Why you will leave, Marcus?
10. Surely you won't sleep, Quintus?

Before doing the next exercises here are a few more 3rd Conjugation verbs to learn:

occido	I kill
ostendo	I show
pello	I drive
reddo	I give back
scribo	I write
traho	I drag

and another adverb useful for the Future tense:

cras	tomorrow

EXERCISE 11.8

1. ego te in atrio cras videbo.
2. mox equum novum tibi ostendam.
3. servi corpus animalis e flumine trahent.
4. cras ad Italiam veniemus.
5. tune mihi pecuniam mox reddes?
6. ante noctem ad montes advenietis.
7. cras epistolam longam ad fratrem scribam.
8. venti navem ducis ad oram celeriter pellent.
9. qualem cibum ad filiam mittes?
10. num senem miserum occides, miles crudelis?

EXERCISE 11.9

Write out these sentences and underline each verb and say what tense it is, and then translate into English.

1. multi pueri in horto ludunt.
2. octo servos in culina video.
3. vox magistri pueros non terrebat.

4.   nox omnibus civibus somnum non dabit.
5.   libertus fessus ante ianuam casae stabat.
6.   alium nuntium ad regem mittam.
7.   num puella flores iuveni reddet?
8.   undasne maris audis, puer?
9.   lux lunae tibi viam ostendet.
10.   iuvenis sagittas militum non timebat.

The **Future Tense** of the verb **sum** is as follows:

ero
eris
erit
erimus
eritis
erunt

This is translated as **"I shall/will be"**

EXERCISE 11.10

1.   mox in Africa erimus.
2.   ubi eris cras, Marce?
3.   difficile erit mihi ad urbem hodie venire.
4.   servi fessi erunt, quod mensas graves portant.
5.   facile erit vobis pecuniam mihi reddere.
6.   mater irata erit, quod pueri in horto iterum ludunt.
7.   cras omnes cives in foro erunt.
8.   tempestas navem in oram mox pellet.
9.   mulieres tristes erunt, quod milites multos iuvenes occident.
10.   quot epistolas ad amicos scribes?

EXERCISE 11.11

1.   We will soon be in the city.
2.   Many cavalry will be in front of the walls.
3.   Will you drag the horse out of the field, slaves?
4.   The guards will not hand over their weapons.
5.   Who will be in the forum tomorrow?

GLADIATORS

The most common and best
known of the shows that took
place in the amphitheatres
were the gladiatorial
contests. The Latin word
gladiator in fact means
"swordsman", and the earliest
gladiators were employed to
fight to the death at a funeral
ceremony, because the men
burying their father wanted
somebody else to keep him
company!!

From this modest, and perhaps strange, beginning **gladiator
shows** developed into popular entertainment. In the latter days
of the Roman republic (see Chapter 6) they were put on by rich
men, voluntarily but usually with the intention of gaining
popularity among the people – and therefore political power.

One of the most famous gladiators was from this period, and was
called **Spartacus**. At this time gladiators were recruited from
tough slaves and prisoners and were often treated very cruelly in
what were euphemistically known as "schools" . Spartacus was
one of these, and in 73BC he led his fellow gladiators in a
rebellion in southern Italy which became so widespread that they
spent two years on the rampage before eventually being beaten
by the Roman army. Spartacus was killed, and 6000 were taken
prisoner and then crucified.

It is perhaps less surprising that this
rebellion was initially so successful than
that there was never again another
rebellion like it. Indeed many men
became gladiators voluntarily, and some
gained fame and even fortune.
Gladiators who fought long and well
could then be granted their freedom if
they were slaves, or could retire from

the arena, if they were already free men. Some gladiators gained great popularity, especially among the women, and there are graffiti to prove it!

There were several different types of gladiator, such as:

mirmillones: so called because of the fish (a **mormyr**) on their helmet; they were often from Gaul and therefore sometimes known as **Galli**.

Samnites: named after the tribe in central Italy, heavily armed and particularly distinguished by a large oblong shield and an axe.

Thraces: armed like Thracians from where they originally came, with a round shield and a short sword or dagger.

secutores: meaning "pursuers" and collective name for the three types described above.

retiarii: the "net-men" who would fight one of the gladiators listed above; besides their nets they would carry a three-pointed lance called a trident and a small dagger, and were only lightly armed.

equites: meaning the "cavalry" these were fighters on horseback.

meridiani: meaning the "midday men" these were lightly armed and often provided an interval around noon between the more serious contests.

We also have evidence that there were a few female gladiators, but, even though they were popular with the **emperor Nero**, most Romans regarded them with amusement or contempt!

Before the shows the gladiators would pause in front of the Imperial Box, and instead of bowing or curtseying like

Wimbledon finalists, they would say **"morituri te salutamus"** – "we who are about to die salute you".

Fighting was usually to the death, but a defeated gladiator could appeal to the finger. He held up his finger admitting defeat and asking for mercy. If the crowd favoured him, they gave the thumbs pressed sign and he left the arena, but, if they gave the thumbs turned sign, then he was killed – amid a fanfare of trumpets!

For most of the time throughout the four centuries of the Roman empire crowd control at these shows was not a problem. There was, however, one major disturbance which is recorded. It took place at a gladiatorial show in AD59 in the amphitheatre at **Pompeii** (which you can still visit today). Nobody knows what started it, but two rival groups of supporters, the Pompeians and their neighbours the Nucerians, began rioting. Troops had to be called in, and when order was at last restored not only the amphitheatre, but also the surrounding streets were littered with dead and wounded! But before you condemn this brutality, you should remember what occasionally happens even today at football matches!

EXERCISE 11.12

1. Write a radio commentary describing a gladiatorial fight.

2. Look carefully at the illustrations of the different types of gladiator, choose two and then draw your own pictures of them.

3. Why do you think that crowd violence occurs before, during or after sporting fixtures? Can anything be done to stop it?

VERBS LIKE CAPIO

12

There is a small group of verbs whose conjugation is a mixture of the 3rd and 4th conjugation endings. The three tenses (**Present, Imperfect and Future**) look exactly like the tenses of **audio**, but the **Infinitive and Imperative** look like those of **rego**.

PRESENT	IMPERFECT	FUTURE
cap**io**	cap**iēbam**	cap**iam**
cap**is**	cap**iēbās**	cap**iēs**
cap**it**	cap**iēbat**	cap**iet**
cap**imus**	cap**iēbamus**	cap**iēmus**
cap**itis**	cap**iēbātis**	cap**iētis**
cap**iunt**	cap**iēbant**	cap**ient**

INFINITIVE   cap**ere**

IMPERATIVE   cap**e**, cap**ite**

There are a few verbs of this type like

capio   I take, capture

You have already met

iacio   I throw

Others include:

facio   I do, make
fugio   I flee, run away
effugio   I escape
conspicio   I catch sight of
cupio   I want, desire

EXERCISE 12.1

1.   capimus.
2.   cupiunt.
3.   fugite.
4.   iacere.

5. effugiebamus.
6. me conspiciet.
7. quid facitis?
8. fugere cupimus.
9. tela iaciebant.
10. urbem capient.

EXERCISE 12.2

1. We are fleeing.
2. He is escaping.
3. They will desire.
4. She was throwing.
5. We catch sight of.
6. Run away at once, Marcus.
7. Throw your spears, soldiers.
8. What are doing, Tullia?
9. She wants to escape.
10. Will you capture the town, Caesar?

EXERCISE 12.3

1. multi milites hastas in hostes iaciunt.
2. post proelium omnes equites fugere cupiebant.
3. nonne me in theatro conspicies, Iulia?
4. num trans montes in Italiam iter facietis?
5. servi mali aurum e casa capiunt.
6. difficile erit per silvas effugere.
7. quid hodie facere cupis, Gai? veni mecum ad amphitheatrum.
8. filia regis cum iuvene ex insula effugere cupit.
9. custodes multa tela in flumen ferociter iaciebant.
10. Graeci urbem Troiam capere diu cupiebant.

EXERCISE 12.4

Rewrite the following sentences, putting the nouns, verbs, adjectives and pronouns into the plural, and then translate into English.

1. miles miser trans montem effugiebat.
2. iace hastam in casam, nauta.
3. senex cum filio ad insulam fugiet.
4. cur te in mare iacere cupis, puer?
5. ego animal ingens in silva conspicio.

Note that the following three verbs have a **shortened singular form** in the **Imperative**.

facio	**fac, facite**
dico	**dic, dicite**
duco	**duc, ducite**

EXERCISE 12.5

1. dic mihi nomen animalis ingentis.
2. duc pueros ad forum, serve.
3. facite mecum iter longum ad Africam, comites.
4. fuge statim, fili, quod hostes celeriter appropinquant.
5. trade arma nobis, miles. num effugere paras?
6. pueri non fessi sunt et aliam fabulam audire cupient.
7. Horatius comites a ponte fugere cogebat.
8. Cloelia et puellae e castris hostium effugiebant.
9. num regina pulchra se occidere cupit?
10. Aeneas multa itinera cum comitibus faciebat.

EXERCISE 12.6

1. We will soon capture the city.
2. The weary slaves want to sleep.
3. Surely the old men won't escape?
4. Take the dog into the garden, Marcus.
5. The naughty boy was throwing a huge rock into the farmer's house.

EXERCISE 12.7

Write two or three Latin sentences to describe what is happening
in this picture.

EXERCISE 12.8

magister ludum intrat. pueri clamant, et Marcus cum Publio
pugnat. subito magistrum vident et statim tacent.

magister: salvete, pueri. sedete.

pueri: salve, magister.

magister: hodie laeti eritis. <u>nihil</u> de militibus vos docebo. nihil
de <u>temporibus</u> antiquis audietis. hodie in amphitheatro sunt
gladiatores noti et <u>bestiae</u> saevae. quis mecum venire cupit?
nonne gladiatores spectare cupitis? num in ludo manebitis?

pueri: ad amphiteatrum tecum venire valde cupimus. quis
hodie pugnat? quales gladiatores videbimus? retiarios et
secutores spectabimus?

magister: omnes gladiatores hodie pugnabunt. bestias quoque
ingentes et feroces videbitis. pugna erit <u>mirabilis</u>.

Marcus: cur <u>hic</u> nunc manemus? amici, e ludo effugite et
festinate mecum ad amphitheatrum. nonne <u>principem</u>
conspiciemus?

nihil	nothing
tempus, temporis (n)	time
bestia, bestiae (f)	wild beast
mirabilis, e	wonderful, amazing
hic	here
princeps, principis (m)	emperor, leader

EXERCISE 12.9

1. The boys want to escape from school.
2. Wait here, Marcus, and say nothing.
3. Many citizens will be in the amphiteatre today.
4. The gladiator was throwing his sword into the crowd.
5. It will be wonderful to catch sight of the emperor.

EXERCISE 12.10

1. Explain the meaning of the following English words, and show how they derive from Latin:

   annihilate   procrastinate   temporal   tractor.

2. Find English derivations from the following Latin words, and write a sentence for each which clearly shows its meaning:

   capio   pello   princeps   traho.

BEAST SHOWS

There was another type of fighter who would perform, in the arena – the **bestiarii**. These were the beast fighters who would take on one or more wild animal, often single-handed. As with other types of gladiator, some of these became very famous, and even emperors such as **Nero** and **Commodus** were known to take on animals in the arena – although the animals were drugged beforehand!!

These trained fighters would take on almost any animal from wild lions to dangerous crocodiles – and such shows still take place today. Not only are there bull fights in Spain and southern

France (as referred to in Chapter 10), but you can see snake shows and crocodile shows in the Far East and other places in the world.

You will no doubt have heard of Christians being thrown to the lions. This did happen not just to Christians but to various slaves and prisoners, and in a later chapter you will read the famous story of **"Androcles and the Lion."**

Not only was beast set against man, but also against one another. At the opening of the **Colosseum** (described in Chapter 10) the emperor **Titus** is said to have had 5000 animals slaughtered in one day! Such animals included lions, tigers,panthers, leopards, hyenas, lynxes, rhinoceroses, hippopotami, zebra, horses, elephants, camels, giraffes, bears, elks, bison, crocodiles, ostriches and antelopes.

Such animals, however, were not always killed. There were other types of show where the animals performed – often in extraordinary ways. We read about monkeys riding chariots driven by goats and elephants giving a dinner party – there is even one tale of elephants trained to walk a tightrope! All kinds of weird and wonderful shows were designed to keep the mob happy.

It was the satirical poet **Juvenal** who cynically and famously remarked that all that was needed to keep the Roman citizen happy was **"panem et circenses"** – "bread and circuses". There may be some truth in this, and certainly there were very many days in the year when the emperor would stage lavish games for the citizens to enjoy.

What is perhaps surprising is that we hear so little condemnation in the Roman world of the various events that took place in the arena. They were most certainly brutal, and they were still being staged well after the Roman empire had become Christian.

The story of **Alypius**, told by **St. Augustine**, the great Christian writer of about AD400, is very illuminating about the all-embracing popularity of the shows in the arena.

> "Alypius had been taken to the arena against his will, but, when they arrived, the whole place was seething with the lust for cruelty. They found seats as best they could, and Alypius shut his eyes tightly, determined to have nothing to do with these atrocities. If only he had closed his ears as well! For an incident in the fight drew a great roar from the crowd, and this thrilled him so deeply that he could not contain his curiosity. Whatever had caused the uproar, he was confident that, if he saw it, he would find it repulsive and remain master of himself. So he opened his eyes and his soul was stabbed with a wound more deadly than that which the gladiator, whom he was so anxious to see, had received in his body. When he saw the blood, it was as though he had drunk a deep draught of savage passion. Instead of turning away, he fixed his eyes on the scene and drank up all its frenzy."

EXERCISE 12.11

1. Imagine you are in ancient Rome and go to see a beast show. Describe what it would be like.

2. Do you think we should condemn the Romans as being cruel nation because of the bloody sports which took place in the arena?

3. Would you stop all blood sports which still go on in the world today?

FOURTH DECLENSION NOUNS

13

There is a small group of Nouns whose **Nominative** ends in **-us** but their declension is different from that of **servus**.

These are known as **4th Declension** Nouns, and this is how they decline:

	SINGULAR	PLURAL
NOM/VOC	man**us**	man**ūs**
ACC	man**um**	man**ūs**
GEN	man**ūs**	man**uum**
DAT	man**uī**	man**ibus**
ABL	man**ū**	man**ibus**

You can see that the **u-** is dominant throughout the declension, except for the **Dat/Abl Plural** which is the same as in the 3rd Declension.

Like the 3rd Declension these nouns can be **Masculine or Feminine**:

e.g.	**manus (f)**	hand
	domus (f)	house, home
	exercitus (m)	army
	impetus (m)	charge, attack
	gradus (m)	step
	portus (m)	harbour
	senatus (m)	senate

There are even fewer **Neuter** nouns of this type, but note the Declension of **genu** (knee).

	SINGULAR	PLURAL
NOM//VOC/ACC	genu	genua
GEN	genūs	genuum
DAT	genu	genibus
ABL	genu	genibus

EXERCISE 13.1

1.   tempestas saeva navem in portu tenet.
2.   in gradibus templi stabamus.
3.   in senatu erant multi viri sapientes.
4.   dux exercitus erat vir fortis et audax.
5.   gradus theatri ascendebamus.
6.   manus agricolae erant ingentes.
7.   revenite domum statim, pueri.
8.   socii alium exercitum ad nos mittunt.
9.   exercitus impetum in hostes mox faciet.
10. mulier in genua ante ducem non cadet.

EXERCISE 13.2

1.   ad portum ante noctem adveniemus.
2.   exercitui hostium est dux crudelis.
3.   duc canem domum, Iulia.
4.   servi regi parent, et in genua statim cadunt.
5.   multi servi in agris manibus laborabant.
6.   venti nos in portum mox pellent, nautae.
7.   in gradibus domus diu sedebamus.
8.   exercitus duci non placet, quod milites non bene pugnant.
9.   cives senatui parere non semper cupiebant.
10. gladiator audax animal saevum gladio vulnerat.

EXERCISE 13.3

1.   The army will soon capture the city.
2.   Do you see the steps of the old temple?
3.   Walk with me to the harbour, Marcus.
4.   The consul's words do not please the senate.

5. We will make another attack on the enemies' camp.

EXERCISE 13.4

In the following sentences underline each noun or pronoun and say what case it is, and then translate each sentence into English.

1. agricola cibum tauro dabit.
2. iuvenes contra hostes manibus pugnabant.
3. exercitus consulum erat ante muros urbis.
4. ego sine comitibus in castra impetum faciam.
5. servi, parate cenam nobis.
6. miles equum ducis gladio necabit.
7. ad oppidum hostium cum sociis festinabimus.
8. tempestas navem regis in portu delet.
9. lux lunae viam exercitui ostendit.
10. o filia, cur tu in genua cadis?

EXERCISE 13.5

Write out Exercise 5.5 but put each of the verbs into the **Imperfect** tense, and then translate into English.

EXERCISE 13.6

poeta, nomine Quintus Horatius Flaccus, per vias urbis ambulat. subito amicum conspicit. amicus est alius poeta, nomine Publius Vergilius Maro.

Horatius: salve, amice. quid portas?

Vergilius: ego carmen novum habeo.

Horatius: carmen mihi lege.

Vergilius: partem modo carminis habeo. carmen est de Aenea, principe Troiano et filio deae Veneris. Aeneas ex urbe Troia cum comitibus effugit et ad Italiam iter facit, quod di Troianos urbem novam ibi aedificare iubent. ego tamen carmen tibi legere non cupio, quod nunc ad theatrum festino. tune mecum venire cupis?

Horatius: quid in theatro videbis? qualem fabulam spectabis?

Vergilius: fabulam Plauti grex actorum hodie dat. fabulas Plauti amo. Plautus de patre, sene gravi, et filio, iuvene non felici, saepe scribit. in fabula semper est servus <u>callidus</u>. servus iuvenem iuvat et a periculis servat.

Horatius: hodie in theatrum venire non cupio. domum <u>enim</u> festinare et carmina scribere debeo.

pars, partis (f)	part
modo	only
ibi	there
callidus, a, um	cunning
enim*	for (giving a reason)

* Note that **enim** can never come first in its sentence or clause

EXERCISE 13.7

1. The poet is writing about the Trojan war.
2. The gods order us to sail to Italy.
3. The cunning slaves escape from the danger.
4. The serious old man does not want to help his son.
5. Why are you hurrying to the theatre, Quintus? Will you watch a play there?

CHARIOT RACING

There was yet another attraction for Romans, and this was **chariot racing**. Feverish excitement accompanied chariot races, and there would be fanatical enthusiasm for the various teams – such as for football teams today.

These races took place in a **circus** – meaning something very different from what that word means today. The Roman circus was oval rather than round, and, like the theatre and amphitheatre and most modern stadiums, was open air.

There were several circuses in the Roman world, but the most famous was the **Circus Maximus** in Rome itself, set in the valley between the Palatine and Aventine hills. As with the Colosseum, you can still see its remains today – you can just wander through and try to imagine what it was like in its heyday.

The **Circus Maximus** was in fact a huge building, in its own way as impressive as the Colosseum. It was originally built in the 4th century BC , but **Augustus** enlarged it to hold up to 250,000 spectators. The arena itself was 600 metres long and 87 metres

wide, and, as with theatres and amphitheatres, the seats were in three tiers. The emperor and his family sat in the **Imperial Box** on the north side, while the **Governor of Rome** had his own special box on the south side. Outside the building there were arcades of shops.

The track itself, like the whole building, was oval and there was a barrier down the middle, called the **spina** – meaning "spine or backbone". The chariots were released from twelve starting gates called **carceres** at a signal from the presiding magistrate (perhaps the emperor himself) who would drop a white cloth called a **mappa**.

The races would be fast and furious, and the most dangerous part came at the turning points. These were marked by three conical posts called **metae**, and crashes were frequent at these turns. The chariots usually had to go seven laps round, which is about two and a half miles. To get a clear understanding of a fierce chariot race you should watch the famous film **Ben Hur**.

There were often as many as twenty-four races in a day. The charioteers were divided into four teams, distinguished by their colours: **the Reds, the Whites, the Blues and the Greens**. Various emperors showed their support for one of these teams, and there were fans both of whole teams as well as of individual charioteers. If any of you are fortunate enough to have visited the horse-race called the **Palio** in **Siena** you will have seen something of the atmosphere which I suspect attended a chariot race in the Circus Maximus.

The **emperor Domitian** was a particular supporter of chariot racing. He added two new teams (**the Golds and the Purples**), and decreased the number of laps from seven to five so that there could be more races in the day. He also built a new circus, which is still visible in Rome's **Piazza Navona** – the name suggests that here, as in the Colosseum, mock naval battles took place.

Piazza Navona

Unlike gladiators, charioteers were free men, and they could earn huge sums of money. To them indeed came fame and fortune, and they enjoyed much of the glamorous lifestyle which modern sports personalities and pop stars can achieve. Some became favourites of the emperor of the time, and could thus gain power and influence.

Perhaps the most famous charioteer of all was a man called **Diocles**. He first rode for the Whites, but then transferred to the Reds – whether for a huge fee we do not know! For those of you who like statistics, Diocles drove chariots for 24 years, during which time he rode in 4,257 races and won 1,462 victories! He is said to have earned a total of 35 million sesterces – it is almost impossible to translate into modern terms, but this would certainly equal several million pounds!

EXERCISE 13. 8

1. Write a radio commentary for a chariot race.

2. Why do you think that chariot racing was so popular in the Roman world? What sports, if any, do you think produce the same excitement today?

3. Persuade your teacher to show you on video the film of Ben Hur and/or Spartacus – you might like to save this up for an end of term treat!

FIFTH DECLENSION NOUNS, TIME

14

There is another, even smaller, group of nouns which belong to what is known as the 5th Declension.

dies (m) = day is one of the few examples, and declines as follows:

	SINGULAR	PLURAL
NOM/VOC	diēs	diēs
ACC	diēm	diēs
GEN	dieī	diērum
DAT	dieī	diēbus
ABL	diē	diēbus

Other such nouns are:

acies (f)	line of battle
fides (f)	faith, loyalty
meridies (m)	midday, noon
res (f)	thing, affair, matter
spes (f)	hope

There are no Neuter nouns in this declension.

EXERCISE 14.1

1. duces de multis rebus diu dicebant.
2. iuvenis multas spes habebat.
3. nonne librum ante meridiem leges, fili?
4. spemne in fide sociorum habes?
5. dux milites e castris ducit et aciem parat.
6. mox de magna re audietis, cives.
7. in acie hostium erant multi senes.
8. post meridiem gladiatores spectabitis, pueri.

9.   mulieres ante acies stabant.

10.   Aeneas reginae fidem non ostendit.

Having learnt the word **dies** (day), you should now see how the Romans expressed different types of **TIME**.

Before doing so, learn/revise these other time words:

tempus,temporis (n)	time
hora, ae (f)	hour
nox, noctis (f)	night
mensis, mensis (m)	month
annus, i (m)	year
prima lux, primae lucis	dawn

Numbers are of course often used in expressions of time. You already know the numbers from 1 to 10; now also learn the Latin words for 1st to 10th:

1	**unus**	1st	**primus**
2	**duo**	2nd	**secundus**
3	**tres**	3rd	**tertius**
4	**quattuor**	4th	**quartus**
5	**quinque**	5th	**quintus**
6	**sex**	6th	**sextus**
7	**septem**	7th	**septimus**
8	**octo**	8th	**octavus**
9	**novem**	9th	**nonus**
10	**decem**	10th	**decimus**

Note that <u>**all** ordinals</u> (first, second, third etc.) decline like **magnus**.

The **ACCUSATIVE** is used to express **TIME HOW LONG**:

tres dies in insula manebamus
We stayed on the island **for three days**

rex **novem annos** regebat
The king was ruling **for nine years**

Sometimes **per** is used together with the **ACCUSATIVE**

> **per septem annos** in urbe habitabamus
> **For seven years** we lived in the city

The **ABLATIVE** is used to express:

a) TIME WHEN

> **sexto die** ex urbe discedemus
> **On the sixth day** we shall leave the city

> **tertia hora** ad ludum adveniemus
> **At the third hour** (i.e. about 9 a.m.) * we will get to school

b) TIME WITHIN WHICH

> **sex diebus** ad urbem reveniemus
> **Within six days/in six days' time** we shall return to the city

> **quinque diebus** urbem delebunt
> **Within five days** they will destroy the city

* You must remember that the Romans lived long before the era of the digital watch and were delightfully vague about time. (They had no trains or planes to catch or video-machines to set!!). Hours were counted not as in our manner, starting at midnight and again at noon, but by sunlight, and this is still done in some parts of Africa today. So when translating into English you must remember that **prima hora** means **the first hour of daylight i.e. about 7 a.m.** and not one o'clock.

It is also useful to remember that **cardinal** numbers **(one, two, three, etc.)** are used in expressions of **time how long** and **time within which**, whereas **ordinal** numbers **(first, second, third etc.)** are used to express **time when**.

EXERCISE 14.2

1. mater pueris fabulas tres horas narrabat.
2. prima luce discedere debetis.
3. sex noctes in silvis nos celabamus.
4. quattuor annis domum revenietis.
5. consules in senatu de re gravi multas horas dicebant.
6. septima hora cenam parabimus.
7. pater in atrio breve tempus manebat.
8. quot menses in urbe habitabas?
9. tempestates naves in portu per tres dies tenebant.
10. decimo anno Graeci urbem Troiam tandem capiunt.

EXERCISE 14.3

1. ego vos in urbe octo diebus videbo.
2. acies ante muros sex horas stabant.
3. ante meridiem ad primam insulam advenies.
4. seni sunt quinque filiae.
5. septem pueri in gradu tertio sedebant.
6. discedite e castris ante primam lucem .
7. novem dies servus miser post casam agricolae se celabat.
8. tertio die domum revenire debes, Iulia.
9. dux quattuor epistolas ad uxorem uno die mittit.
10. decem gladiatores tres horas fortiter pugnabant.

EXERCISE 14.4

1. The children were sitting under the trees for three hours.
2. The army destroys ten towns in five days.
3. On the fourth day I shall return to the island.
4. We shall talk about the serious matters for five days.
5. Surely you will leave before midday?

EXERCISE 14.5

Write out Exercise 5.6 but put each of the verbs into the **Future** tense, and then translate into English.

EXERCISE 14.6

hodie est <u>dies festus</u>. pueri ad ludum festinant. in atrio patrem exspectant.

Marcus: quid hodie faciemus?

Iulia: domi manere amo. in hortum errabo et sub umbra arborum multas horas sedebo. librum novum legam. tune in hortum venire cupis?

Marcus: ego in Circum Maximum iter facere cupio. nonne tu mecum venire cupis, Iulia?

Iulia: ego quoque Circum Maximum amo. <u>aurigas</u> spectare amo.

pater atrium intrat. filium filiamque salutat.

pater: hodie per vias urbis ad Circum Maximum celeriter ambulabimus. manete mecum. in via enim erunt multi viri, multae mulieres, multi pueri, multi servi. omnes ad Circum Maximum festinabunt.

pater cum Marco Iuliaque portas Circi Maximi intrant. prope arenam sedent, quod pater est <u>senator</u> Romanus.

Marcus: ecce, princeps signum dat. aurigae equos ferociter agunt. ad metam celeriter appropinquant. quis cadet? ecce, duo aurigae ad terram nunc cadunt. equi sine aurigis per circum saeve currunt.

post tres horas senator cum filio filiaque domum revenit. omnes fessi sunt, sed laeti.

dies festus	holiday
auriga, aurigae (m)	charioteer
senator, senatoris (m)	senator
ago (3)	I drive

EXERCISE 14.7

1. What do you want to do today, Marcus?
2. Wait for father in the atrium, children.
3. Julia and Marcus were hurrying through the gates of the circus.
4. The senator wishes to watch all the charioteers.
5. The weary horse slowly falls to the ground.

EXERCISE 14.8

1. Explain the meaning of the following English words, and show how they derive from Latin:

    edifice   genuflect   gradual   impetuous

2. Find English derivations from the following Latin words, and write a sentence for each which clearly shows its meaning:

    annus   decimus   festus   nox

THE BATHS

When the Romans were not rushing off to watch chariot races, gladiatorial shows or plays, they might otherwise spend their leisure time by going to relax at **the baths**.

There are many references to baths in Latin literature, and much has also been discovered from the many remains which survive throughout the Roman Empire. Among the most famous are the **Baths of Caracalla** (a Roman emperor of the 3rd century AD) which you can still see in Rome, and also in Rome the Baths of another emperor, **Diocletian**, have now become the National Museum.

As in this country until about eighty years ago, so in the ancient Roman world only the rich could afford private baths within their own homes. These existed in both town houses and in country villas, and in a rich property there might even be bathing arrangements for the slaves.

Yet for the majority, the rich as well as the poor, bathing would take place in public baths. These were called **thermae** or **balneae**, and the most famous in Britain are at **Bath**, which of course derives its name from them.

At Bath, as in many other places, the baths were built around existing hot springs. Where these did not exist, the baths were heated by a **hypocaust**. These conducted hot air from a furnace under the floor and through vents and ducts in the walls. The fuel for the furnace was wood and charcoal, which of course slaves had to work.

Once at the baths, people would move from room to room, according to temperature. First they would go to the changing room (**apodyterium**) to leave their clothes; then to the cold room (**frigidarium**) for a cold plunge bath, and after that the warm room (**tepidarium**) to acclimatise themselves before going into the really hot room (**caldarium**). This would be like a modern sauna, and especially like the public baths which still exist in **Turkey**.

Certainly Romans of all classes seemed to spend time at the baths, and the entrance fee was a mere **quadrans** – the smallest Roman coin, and perhaps equivalent to the farthing which used to exist in this country. Children were admitted free.

Many public baths had separate facilities for men and women, or established different hours for them. Mixed bathing, however, does seem to have taken place in some of the baths, but no doubt women who were careful of their reputation did not frequent the baths at all!

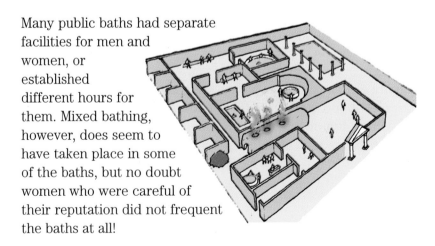

People would have to take certain items with them - not only towels, but also bottles of oil to rub in after bathing, and an implement to wipe the oil off their bodies called a **strigil**. The rich would have slaves to attend on them, but services could be hired at the baths, including barbers, masseurs and attendants to guard the clothes in the changing room.

The Romans would come here not merely to wash, but also for exercise and social life. The baths provided not merely the opportunity to bathe, but to indulge in other exercise too. There were areas for gymnastics and wrestling, and even for ball games. Some of the larger bathing complexes also had gardens, refreshment bars and even libraries. In fact they were not dissimilar to the modern sports clubs which have become so popular in this country in recent years.

EXERCISE 14.9

1. Imagine that you are Marcus or Julia, and describe a visit to the Baths.

2. Why do you think that the Baths were so popular in the Roman world?

3. Plan a visit, if you can, with your family or your school to Bath to explore the Roman baths there.

PLACE; THE LOCATIVE

15

In the last chapter we discussed expressions of **TIME**; we shall now move on to expressions of **PLACE**.

In most instances expressions of **PLACE** involve **prepositions** – as learnt in Chapter 11 of Book 1 and Chapter 1 of this book.

The **ACCUSATIVE** is always used with **prepositions expressing MOTION TO**, and the **ABLATIVE** is always used with **prepositions expressing PLACE AT** and **PLACE FROM**.

Here is a list of prepositions followed by the **ACCUSATIVE**, most of which you already know; now is a good time to revise them and to learn any new ones:

ad	to, towards
ante	before, in front of
circum	around
contra	against
in	into, on to, against
inter	among, between
per	through
post	after, behind
prope	near
propter	on account of, because of
super	over, above
trans	across

Here now is a list of prepositions followed by the **ABLATIVE** for you to learn/revise:

a, ab	from
cum	(together) with
de	1) down from
	2) about (i.e. talk 'about' etc)
e, ex	from, out of
in	in, on
pro	1) in front of
	2) for, on behalf of
sine	without
sub	under

Particular care must be taken of **in** which means **into, on to** when followed by the **ACCUSATIVE** but **in, on** when followed by the **ABLATIVE**

So   in urbe**m** ambulamus
We are walking **into** the city

but   in urb**e** manemus
We stay **in** the city

EXERCISE 15.1

1. pueri fessi sub arboribus multas horas iacebant.
2. septem diebus ad castra hostium adveniemus.
3. propter ventum naves in portu diu manebant.
4. milites pro patria fortiter pugnabant.
5. subito puer de arbore ad terram cadit.
6. senex villam novam prope flumen aedificare cupit.
7. servi trans montes celeriter fugiebant.
8. pater vinum in mensam ponet.
9. in mensa agricolae erant cibus et aqua.
10. multi cives ante portas amphitheatri quattuor horas stabant.

N.B. The simple prepositions meaning **to, from, in** are <u>not used with the names of towns or small islands.</u>

Instead the name of the place is put into the **ACCUSATIVE** for **MOTION TO** and the **ABLATIVE** for **MOTION FROM**.

So   **Romam** veniemus
      We will come **to** Rome

      Londinio cras discedam
      I will depart **from** London tomorrow

This is also true with a few other nouns such as **domus** (house) which you met in the last chapter, and note how English omits the word "to" with this word:

      festina **domum**
      Hurry **home**

With such nouns an old case no longer used with other nouns is used to express **PLACE AT** – this is called the **LOCATIVE**.

The basic ending of this case is **-i**, but in 1st Declension Nouns it combines with **a** to become **-ae**. These endings are best learnt by example and they are also found with certain other common nouns listed below:

Romae	at Rome
Londinii	in London
domi	at home
humi	on the ground
ruri*	in the country(side)
vesperi*	in the evening

* the Ablative forms **rure** and **vespere** are sometimes also found.

For plural nouns the Locative ending is the same as the Ablative:

e.g.   **Athenis**   at Athens

EXERCISE 15.2

1.   ego Romae octo dies manebo.
2.   nono die Roma discedam et Brundisium iter faciam.
3.   ad Graeciam navigabo, sed quinque mensibus Romam reveniam.
4.   post proelium agricola hastas humi invenit.
5.   poeta notus villam ingentem ruri aedificabat.

6. Athenis sunt multa templa pulchra.
7. vesperi senes de multis rebus inter se dicebant.
8. tune Londinium sine fratre iter facies?
9. cur stant mulieres prope balneas?
10. quot annos Londinii manebis, Tullia?

EXERCISE 15.3

1. sol calidus omnes flores in gradibus villae delet.
2. quinto die dux exercitum in castra mittere constituit.
3. cur in horto quattuor horas manebas, Gai? quid faciebas?
4. tertio mense hostes feroces oppidum capiunt.
5. iuvenis cum sex puellis Athenas iter faciet.
6. num super montem ascendere times, frater?
7. est ira inter milites, quod dux iterum pugnare cupit.
8. propter tempestatem pueri domi manere debent.
9. vosne mecum ad insulam post meridiem navigabitis?
10. dux corpus hostis circum muros urbis trahebat.

EXERCISE 15.4

Write two or three Latin sentences to describe what is happening in the picture below.

EXERCISE 15.5

1.   I shall make a journey to Rome within five days.
2.   Will you come with me to London tomorrow, Marcus?
3.   The consul was staying in the country for three months.
4.   I shall stay at home with my friends after dinner.
5.   In the evening we like to sit under the trees.

EXERCISE 15.6

ANDROCLES AND THE LION

Androcles erat servus et in Africa habitabat. servo misero erat <u>dominus</u> crudelis. tandem a domino fugere constituit*. in <u>spelunca</u> se celat. subito in speluncam venit <u>leo</u> ingens. servus valde timet. <u>neque</u> corpus <u>neque</u> manus movet. leo tamen ad servum non ferociter sed lente appropinquat et <u>pedem</u> ostendit.

Androcles pedem leonis spectat et <u>spinam</u> ingentem videt. spinam e pede trahit et leonem curat. in spelunca multos menses laete habitant, sed uno die milites Romani leonem servumque capiunt.

dominus Androclem Romam mittit et milites iubet servum ad bestias iacere. Androclus Romam venit et paucis diebus in arenam inter alios servos lente ambulat. leones sunt ingentes et saevi. sed cur leo servum non oppugnat? cur leo Androclem diu spectat? num est leo amicus servi?

* **Note how Latin switches from the Past to the Present tense. you can either change in English as well, or continue with the Past tense.**

dominus, domini (m)	master
spelunca, specluncae (f)	cave
leo, leonis (m)	lion
neque ... neque	neither ... nor
pes, pedis (m)	foot
spina	(here means) thorn

EXERCISE 15.7

responde Latine:

1. quis erat Androcles?
2. ubi habitabat Androcles?
3. cur Androcles a domino fugere constituit?
4. ubi se celat?
5. quid leo Androcli ostendit?

EXERCISE 15.8

1. The master sends the slaves to Rome.
2. We decide to run away from the lion.
3. The huge animal was slowly moving his foot.
4. The soldiers will capture many wild beasts within one day.
5. Surely the lion will attack the slave?

ENEMIES OF ROME (1)

In this book you have read both about the early legends of Rome, and then about life and literature in the later period of Roman history. Throughout Rome's long history, she became extremely powerful, but at various stages she did have enemies who were jealous of this growing power or who later were trying to attack her vast empire.

At first these enemies were the other peoples living close to Rome, such as the **Etruscans** and the **Volscians**, mentioned in the stories about **Horatius** and **Coriolanus**. However, as Rome's influence spread first throughout Italy and then right across the lands of the Mediterranean, her enemies came from further afield.

The most famous of these was **Hannibal**. He came from the city of **Carthage**, the same city that the legendary **Dido** was supposed to have ruled. By the middle of the third century BC Rome and Carthage were fierce rivals in the western Mediterranean, each of them wanting power and influence in Spain, Sardinia and Sicily.

Almost inevitably, the Romans and the Carthaginians came to fight a war – which the Romans won. A generation later Hannibal, a Carthaginian general, was determined to fight another war against Rome and to take revenge for the previous defeat which Carthage had suffered at her hands – rather like in 1939 Hitler leading Germany into the Second World War to take revenge for what had happened in the First.

Hannibal decided not to lead an attack on Rome by the most direct route, but instead he crossed from Carthage into Spain and then – remarkably – led his vast army (which included **elephants**!) first across the **Pyrenees mountains**, then the **river Rhone**, and finally – most dramatically of all – across the **Alps**.

Having achieved these amazing feats, Hannibal then defeated the Romans in three battles in three successive years. It seemed that Rome would be captured, but two things happened to save the city. First, one of the Roman consuls decided to avoid any further battles since another defeat seemed so likely, and second, Hannibal, instead of attacking Rome and laying siege, dallied in Italy for so long that his troops became bored and he was then recalled home.

By this time there was a new young general called **Scipio**. He led an army across to Africa and defeated the Carthaginians at the battle of **Zama**. Hannibal was later forced to leave Carthage, and subsequently committed suicide. Scipio, however, received great honours in Rome and was given the **cognomen** (i.e extra name) **Africanus** to commemorate his great victory over one of Rome's most formidable enemies. This is rather like General Montgomery gaining the title **Montgomery of Alamein** after winning a great battle there (also in North Africa) against the Germans in World War II.

EXERCISE 15.9

1.   From the maps above make your own map showing Hannibal's route from Carthage to Rome.

2.   Do you think that, if Hannibal had defeated Rome, there would have been a Carthaginian empire just as there had been a Roman empire? If this had happened, you would not now be learning Latin – but perhaps Carthaginian!!

MORE PRONOUNS

16

In Chapter 7 you learnt the Personal Pronouns, the Latin words for **"me" "you" , "us"**.

You know from various examples since early in Book 1 that normally Latin does not use words for **"my" "your"** etc. if they refer back to the subject of the sentence.

e.g.	mater filium amat
means	The mother loves her son

However, there are words which are used:

either	**1) for emphasis**
or	**2) if the "my" "your" etc. does not refer back to the subject of the sentence**

These words are

meus	my
tuus	your (singular)
noster	our
vester	your (plural)

meus, tuus decline like **magnus**
noster, vester decline like **pulcher**

So   hodie **meum** librum habeo
Today I have **my own** book

Marcus **meum** librum habet
Marcus has **my** book

There is also **suus** meaning **"his, her, its, their"**

BUT **suus** can ONLY refer back to subject, and is normally used for emphasis:

So   Marcus librum habet
        Marcus has his book

But   Marcus librum **suum** habet
        Marcus has **his own** book

EXERCISE 16.1

1. cur Publius tuam tabulam habet, Gai?
2. Publius meam tabulam habet, quod suam non invenit.
3. Publi, pete tuam tabulam statim.
4. noster pater est poeta notus.
5. sororem meam in foro hodie videbis, Marce.
6. frater vester mecum Londinii tres menses manebat.
7. tempestas ingens navem nostram non delebit.
8. exercitus noster impetum in castra hostium mox faciet.
9. clamores tuae senem miserum terrent.
10. cur mater vestra Athenas iter facit?

Note how sometimes these pronouns can be used as nouns:

e.g   **nostri**   our men
        sui   his/their men/family

EXERCISE 16.2

1. nostri impetum in hostes subito faciunt.
2. dux suos e nave celeriter mittit.
3. cur tu mea verba non audis, Marce?
4. pater meus novem servos Londinium secum ducit.
5. hostes tela in nostros audacter iaciebant.
6. Caesar suos ad oppidum secundo die ducet.
7. num nautae nostram casam igni delebunt?
8. nostri prope pontem sex dies manebant.
9. soror tua corpora multorum leonum in arena videbit.
10. frater meus te in theatro tres horas exspectabat.

EXERCISE 16.3

1.   Where is your sister, Marcus?
2.   The king sends his own son to the island.
3.   Our ship will wait in the harbour for three days.
4.   Your poem is good, boys.
5.   Caesar was leading his men out of the camp.

There are also some 3rd Person Pronouns meaning **"he, she, him, etc.".** One is **is, ea, id** whose declension you should now learn:

SINGULAR

	MASCULINE	FEMININE	NEUTER
NOM	is	ea	id
ACC	eum	eam	id
GEN	eius	eius	eius
DAT	eī	eī	eī
ABL	eō	eā	eō

PLURAL

	MASCULINE	FEMININE	NEUTER
NOM	eī	eae	ea
ACC	eōs	eas	ea
GEN	eōrum	eārum	eōrum
DAT	eīs	eīs	eīs
ABL	eīs	eīs	eīs

eum monebo
I will warn **him**

eas iuvo
I am helping **them**

Note the difference between these pronouns and **se**:

se ALWAYS refers back to the subject
eum, eam etc NEVER do.

So	**eos** vulnero
	I wound **them**

But	**se** vulnerant
	They wound **themselves**

The genitive of **is, ea, id** is used to mean **"his/their"** referring to somebody else. Again contrast this use with **suus**.

So	voces **eorum** me terrent
	Their voices frighten me

	matrem **eius** iuvo
	I am helping **his** mother

But	matrem **suam** non iuvat
	He does not help **his own** mother

EXERCISE 16.4

1. ubi sunt pueri? pete eos in horto.
2. pater eius est vir fortis.
3. senex fessus est. da ei cibum et aquam.
4. leones nos oppugnant, sed ab eis fugiemus.
5. nonne audis clamores eorum?
6. mulier filios ab hostibus servare cupit. eos in silva celat.
7. post proelium octo milites prope montes se celant.
8. Publius e ludo discedit. ambula domum cum eo, serve.
9. meus frater domi manere cupit, sed Romam sine eo iter facere non amo.
10. leo pedem servo ostendit, quod in eo est magna spina.

is, ea, id can also be used as an adjective meaning **"this"** or **"that"**

e.g.	**eam puellam** spectamus
	We are watching **that girl**

	da pecuniam **eis civibus**
	Give money **to those citizens**

EXERCISE 16.5

1. in ea villa est magnum triclinium pulchrum.
2. dux eos milites ad montes altos mittet.
3. agricola gregem ex eo agro ducebat.
4. tempestas eas naves non delebit.
5. vox eius puellae magistro valde placet.
6. senatus de ea re multos dies dicet.
7. in eo oppido sunt quattuor templa et unum theatrum.
8. portate eam mensam in hortum, servi.
9. ab ea terra sine mora discedemus.
10. duc eum canem ad ripam tecum, Marce.

Now is a good time to note that a few of the adjectives which you have already learnt have a **Genitive and Dative Singular (Masculine, Feminine and Neuter)** like **eius, ei**.

These include:	**alius**	another
	alter	the other
	solus	only, alone
	totus	whole
	unus	one

So pater **alterius consulis**
The father **of the other consul**

da pecuniam **uni puero**
Give money **to one** boy

Note too that **alius** has a **Nom/Acc Neuter Sing** ending in **-d: aliud**

aedificate **aliud theatrum**
Build **another theatre**

EXERCISE 16.6

1. hostes magnam partem totius urbis igni delebant.
2. puer aliud animal in montibus invenit.
3. num cenam uni iuveni paras, Iulia?
4. da id vinum seni soli, serve.

5.   corpus unius leonis in arena manet.
6.   tertio die alia navis Athenas adveniet.
7.   quinque diebus aliud iter Londinium faciemus.
8.   dic nihil alteri consuli de ea re.
9.   uno die in eo theatro tres fabulas spectabitis.
10. miles alterum oculum regis sagitta vulnerat.

EXERCISE 16.7

1.   These winds will destroy the whole harbour.
2.   Give this book to the other boy.
3.   There will soon be another war in this land.
4.   I shall walk to that town with one companion.
5.   The slaves will give this food to one soldier.

EXERCISE 16.8

Hannibal magnum exercitum per Hispaniam ducit. multa oppida capit. trans montes et flumina suos ducit. nunc Romam etiam trans Alpes suos ducere parat. milites tamen timent.

Hannibal: vos, milites, neque hostes neque montes timere debetis. mox in Italia eritis et omnes gentes vincetis.

miles primus: dux, nos eos montes altos ascendere non cupimus. num elephantos super montes duces?

Hannibal: nonne ea animalia ingentia Romanos et alias gentes Italiae valde terrebunt? nos elephantos sine mora trans Alpes ducemus et paucis annis omnes de ea re mirabili dicent.

miles secundus: nonne montes etiam elephantos terrebunt? ei sunt feroces et ingentes, sed montes tam altos timebunt.

Hannibal: nos non timemus, milites. milites mei sunt fortes et audaces, mea animalia quoque sunt fortia et audacia. vos omnes ad multas victorias ducam. milites Romani non bene pugnant. eis sunt duces mali. ego urbem Romam capere paro. eam urbem et totam Italiam regere cupio.

etiam	even
tam	such
victoria, victoriae (f)	victory

EXERCISE 16.9

1. The large army will capture many towns and cities.
2. Surely we will not fight against these huge animals?
3. The brave soldiers were not afraid to climb the high mountains.
4. Our leader is preparing to fight on the third day.
5. We shall speak about these amazing events for many years.

ENEMIES OF ROME (2)

After Rome's war with **Hannibal** she proceeded to gain even more power and influence all round the Mediterranean. In the middle of the first century BC she fought a third war with **Carthage**, which she also won, and at the same time reduced **Greece** to the status of a Roman province. Rome was now mistress of the Mediterranean world, and her leaders began to look even further afield for more conquest.

Probably the most famous Roman general of all is **Julius Caesar**, about whom you have already learnt something. He conquered **Gaul**, and even visited Britain – as well as briefly invading **Germany**. If we are to believe a certain series of books, Caesar did not conquer all of Gaul – there was one small village …

In fact, although **Asterix** is of course a fictional character, yet his name is realistic. There was a Gallic leader called **Vercingetorix**, who led a fierce resistance against Caesar. He was undoubtedly Caesar's most formidable enemy during the **Gallic Wars**, and he organised a widespread revolt amongst the tribes of Gaul, which was very nearly successful. He won several victories before being at last defeated by the might of Caesar and his army, and then only after a long siege.

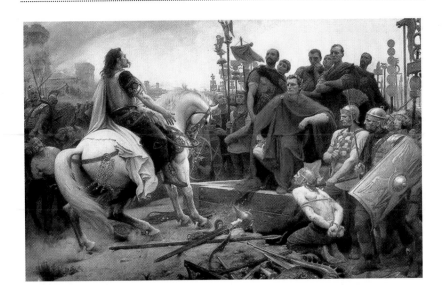

It was customary for Roman leaders to parade their conquered enemies in their triumphal parades back in Rome. This is what happened to Vercingetorix. The same thing happened a century later to the British chieftain, **Caratacus**, who had held out against the army of the **emperor Claudius** until at last being defeated. He was in fact only captured after he had been betrayed by another British ruler – so much for loyalty! Of course several defeated enemies took their own lives rather than suffer the humiliation of defeat: one such was the British queen, **Boudicca**, about whom you read something in the previous book. Another was **Cleopatra**, queen of Egypt.

For four more centuries Rome continued to rule her empire very successfully. Gradually, however, there were new enemies at her borders: peoples like **the Saxons, the Visigoths – and the Vandals**, from whom we get the modern word! It was enemies such as these who finally brought the end of the Roman empire in the fifth century AD, but Rome's power had by now lasted for nearly a thousand years, far, far longer than empires of the modern period – a truly remarkable achievement!

EXERCISE 16.10

1.   Draw a picture of how you imagine a battle involving the Romans and her enemies would have been.

2.   Why do think Rome attracted enemies?

3.   Do you think that it was inevitable that the Roman empire came to an end?

VOCABULARY

LATIN–ENGLISH

a, ab + Abl	from
ad + Acc	to, towards
advenio (4)	I arrive (at)
aedifico (1)	I build
ager, agri (m)	field
agricola, agricolae (m)	farmer
alius, a, ud	(an)other
alter, era, erum	the other (of two)
altus, a, um	high, deep
ambulo (1)	I walk
amicus, amici (m)	friend
amo (1)	I love, like
amphitheatrum,	
amphitheatri (n)	amphitheatre
animal, animalis (n)	animal
annus, anni (m)	year
ante + Acc	before, in front of
antiquus, a, um	old, ancient
appropinquo (1)	I approach
aqua, aquae (f)	water
arbor, arboris (f)	tree
arena, arenae (f)	sand, arena
arma, armorum (n.pl)	arms, weapons
ascendo (3)	I climb
atrium, atrii (n)	entrance-hall
audax, audacis	bold, daring
audio (4)	I hear, listen to
aurum, auri (n)	gold
auxilium, auxilii (n)	help

balneae, balnearum (f.pl)	baths
bellum, belli (n)	war
bene	well
bonus, a, um	good
brevis, e	short
cado (3)	I fall
caelum, caeli (n)	sky, heaven
calidus, a, um	hot
callidus, a, um	cunning
canis, canis (m/f)	dog
canto (1)	I sing
capio (3)	I capture
caput, capitis (n)	head
carmen, carminis (n)	song, poem
casa, casae (f)	house
castra, castrorum (n.pl)	camp
celeriter	quickly
celo (1)	I hide
cena, cenae (f)	dinner
cibus, cibi (m)	food
circum + Acc	around
civis, civis (m/f)	citizen
clamo (1)	I shout
clamor, clamoris (m)	shout
cogo (3)	I force, compel
comes, comitis (m/f)	companion
conspicio (3)	I catch sight of
constituo (3)	I decide
consul, consulis (m)	consul
contra + Acc	against
corpus, corporis (n)	body
cras	tomorrow
crudelis, e	cruel
culina, culinae (f)	kitchen
cum + Abl	with
cupio (3)	I wish, want, desire
cur?	why?
curo (1)	I look after
curro (3)	I run
custos, custodis (m/f)	guard

de + Abl	about, down from
dea, deae (f)	goddess
debeo (2)	I ought to, must
decem	ten
decimus, a, um	tenth
deinde	then
deleo (2)	I destroy
descendo (3)	I go down
deus, dei (m)	god
dico (3)	I say, speak, tell
dies, diei (m)	day
difficilis, e	difficult
discedo (3)	I depart, leave
diu	for a long time
do (1)	I give
doceo (2)	I teach
doleo (2)	I grieve
dominus, domini (m)	master
domus, domus (f)	home
dormio (4)	I sleep
duco (3)	I lead, take
dulcis, e	sweet
duo	two
dux, ducis (m/f)	leader, guide
e, ex + Abl	out of
ecce	look!
effugio (3)	I escape
ego	I
enim	for (because)
epistola, epistolae (f)	letter
equites, equitum (m.pl)	cavalry
equus, equi (m)	horse
erro (1)	I wander
et	and
et .. et	both ... and
etiam	even, also
exercitus, exercitus (m)	army
exspecto (1)	I wait for

fabula, fabulae (f)	story, play
facilis, e	easy
facio (3)	I do, make
felix, felicis	lucky, happy
femina, femiae (f)	woman
ferox, ferocis	fierce
fessus, a, um	tired
festino (1)	I hurry
fides, fidei (f)	faith, loyalty
filia, filiae (f)	daughter
filius, filii (m)	son
fleo (2)	I weep
flos, floris (m)	flower
flumen, fluminis (n)	river
fortis, e	brave
forum, fori (n)	forum, market-place
frater, fratris (m)	brother
fugio (3)	I flee, run away
gens, gentis (f)	race, tribe, family
genu, genus (n)	knee
gladius (m)	sword
gradus, gradus (m)	step
gravis, e	heavy, serious
grex, gregis (m)	flock, herd, company of actors
habeo (2)	I have
habito (1)	I live (in)
hasta, hastae (f)	spear
hic	here
hodie	today
hortus, horti (m)	garden
hostis, hostis, (m/f)	enemy
iaceo (2)	I lie down
iacio (3)	I throw
iam	now, already
ianua, ianuae (f)	door
ibi	there
igitur	therefore
ignis, ignis (m)	fire

impetus, impetus (m)	force, attack
in + Abl	in, on
in + Acc	into, on to
incola, incolae (m/f)	inhabitant
ingens, ingentis	huge
inquit (3)	he/she says
insula, insulae (f)	island, block of flats
inter + Acc	among, between
intro (1)	I enter
invenio (4)	I find
ira, irae (f)	anger
iratus, a, um	angry
is, ea, id	1) he/she/it
	2) this, that
itaque	and so, therefore
iter, itineris (n)	journey
iterum	again
iubeo (2)	I order
iuvenis, iuvenis (m)	young man
iuvo (1)	I help
laboro (1)	I work
laetus, a, um	happy
laudo (1)	I praise
lectus, lecti (m)	couch, bed
lego (3)	I read
lente	slowly
leo, leonis (m)	lion
liber, libri (m)	book
libertus, liberti (m)	freedman
longe	far
longus, a, um	long
ludo (3)	I play
ludus, ludi (m)	school
luna, lunae (f)	moon
lux, lucis (f)	light
magister, magistri (m)	schoolmaster
magnus, a, um	big, large, great
malus, a, um	bad

maneo (2)	I stay, wait
manus, manus (f)	hand
mare, maris (n)	sea
mater, matris (f)	mother
matrimonium,	
matrimonii (n)	marriage
mensa, mensae (f)	table
mensies, mensies (m)	month
meridies, meridiei (m)	midday
meus, a, um	my
miles, militis (m/f)	soldier
miser, era, erum	miserable, wretched
mitto (3)	I send
moneo (2)	I warn, advise
mons, montis (m)	mountain
monstro (1)	I show, point out
mora, morae (f)	delay
moveo (2)	I move
mox	soon
mulier, mulieris (f)	woman
multi, ae, a	many
murus, muri (m)	wall
narro (1)	I tell
nato (1)	I swim
nauta, nautae (m)	sailor
navigo (1)	I sail
navis, navis (f)	ship
-ne?	?
neco (1)	I kill
neque ... neque	neither ... nor
nescio (4)	I do not know
nihil	nothing
non	not
nonne?	surely?
nonus, a, um	ninth
nos	we, us
noster, tra, trum	our
novem	nine
novus, a, um	new

nox, noctis (f)	night
num?	surely not?
nunc	now
nuntius, nuntii (m)	messenger, message
occido (3)	I kill
occupo (1)	I seize
octavus, a, um	eighth
octo	eight
oculus, oculi (m)	eye
omnis, e	every, all
oppidum, oppidi (n)	town
oppugno (1)	I attack
ora, orae (f)	shore
oro (1)	I beg
ostendo (3)	I show
pareo (2) + Dat	I obey
paro (1)	I prepare
pars, partis (f)	part
parvus, a, um	small, little
pater, patris (m)	father
patria, patriae (f)	own country/city
pecunia, pecuniae (f)	money
pello (3)	I drive
per + Acc	through
periculum, periculi (n)	danger
pes, pedis (m)	foot
peto (3)	I seek, make for, ask for
placeo (2) + Dat	I please
poeta, poetae (m)	poet
pono (3)	I put, place
pons, pontis (m)	bridge
porto (1)	I carry
portus, portus (m)	harbour
post + Acc	after, behind
primus, a, um	first
princeps, principis (m)	leader, chief, emperor
pro + Abl	on behalf of
proelium, proelii (n)	battle

prope + Acc	near
propter + Acc	on account of
puella, puellae (f)	girl
puer, pueri (m)	boy
pugno (1)	I fight
pulcher, ra, rum	beautiful
qualis, e?	what kind of?
quartus, a, um	fourth
quattuor	four
quid?	what?
quinque	five
quintus, a, um	fifth
quis?	who?
quod	because
quoque	also
quot?	how many?
reddo (3)	I give back
regina, reginae (f)	queen
rego (3)	I rule
res, rei (f)	thing, affair, matter, event
respondeo (2)	I reply, answer
rex, regis (m)	king
ripa, ripae (f)	river-bank
rogo (1)	I ask
rus, ruris (n)	country(side)
saepe	often
saevus, a, um	fierce, savage
sagitta, sagittae (f)	arrow
saluto (1)	I greet
salve(te)	hello!, greetings!
sapiens, sapientis	wise
saxum, saxi (n)	rock , stone
scio (4)	I know
scribo (3)	I write
se	himself/herself/themselves
secundus. a, um	second
sed	but
sedeo (2)	I sit

semper	always
senator, senatoris (m)	senator
senatus, senatus (m)	senate
senex, senis (m)	old man
septem	seven
septimus, a, um	seventh
servo (1)	I keep safe
servus, servi (m)	slave
sex	six
sextus. a, um	sixth
signum, signi (n)	signal
silva, silvae (f)	wood
sine + Abl	without
socius, socii (m)	ally
sol, solis (m)	sun
solus, a, um	alone, only
somnus, somni (m)	sleep
soror, sororis (f)	sister
specto (1)	I look at
spes, spei (f)	hope
statim	at once, immediately
sto (1)	I stand
subito	suddenly
super + Acc	over, on top of
supero (1)	I overcome
suus, a, um	his/her/its/their own
tabula, tabulae (f)	writing-tablet
taceo (2)	I am silent
tam	so, such
tamen	however
tandem	at last
taurus (m)	bull
telum, teli (n)	weapon
tempestas, tempestatis (f)	storm
templum, templi (n)	temple
tempus, temporis (n)	time
teneo (2)	I hold
terreo (2)	I frighten

tertius, a, um	third
theatrum, theatri (n)	theatre
thermae,	
thermarum (f.pl)	baths
timeo (2)	I fear, am afraid of
trado (3)	I hand over
traho (3)	I drag
trans + Acc	across
tres	three
triclinium, triclinii (n)	dining-room
tu	you (singular)
turba, turbae (f)	crowd
tutus, a, um	safe
tuus, a, um	your (sing)
ubi?	where?
umbra, umbrae (f)	shade
unda, undae (f)	wave
unus, a, um	one
urbs, urbis (f)	city
uxor, uxoris, (f)	wife
valde	very (much)
validus, a, um	strong
venio (4)	I come
ventus, venti (m)	wind
verbum, verbi (n)	word
vesper, vesperi (m)	evening
vester, tra, trum	your (plural)
veto (1)	I forbid
via, viae (f)	road, way
video (2)	I see
villa, villae (f)	country-house
vinco (3)	I defeat, conquer
vinum, vini (n)	wine
vir, viri (m)	man, husband
voco (1)	I call
vos	you (plural)
vox, vocis (f)	voice
vulnero (1)	I wound
vulnus, vulneris (n)	wound

ENGLISH–LATIN

about	**de + Abl**
across	**trans + Acc**
afraid, I am	**timeo (2)**
after	**post + Acc**
again	**iterum**
against	**contra + Acc**
all	**omnes**
ally	**socius, socii (m)**
alone	**solus, a, um**
already	**iam**
also	**quoque, etiam**
always	**semper**
among	**inter + Acc**
amphitheatre	**amphitheatrum, amphitheatri (n)**
ancient	**antiquus, a, um**
and	**et**
and so	**itaque**
anger	**ira, irae (f)**
angry	**iratus, a, um**
animal	**animal, animalis (n)**
approach, I	**appropinquo (1)**
arms	**arma, armorum (n.pl)**
army	**exercitus, exercitus (m)**
around	**circum + Acc**
arrive (at), I	**advenio (4)**
arrow	**sagitta, sagittae (f)**
ask, I	**rogo (1)**
ask for, I	**peto (3)**
at last	**tandem**
at once	**statim**
attack	**impetus, impetus (m)**
attack, I	**oppugno (1)**
bad	**malus, a, um**
baths	**balneae, balneaarum (f.pl)**
	thermae, thermarum (f.pl)
battle	**proelium, proelii (n)**
beautiful	**pulcher, ra, rum**

because	**quod**
before	**ante + Acc**
beg, I	**oro (1)**
behind	**post + Acc**
between	**inter + Acc**
big	**magnus, a, um**
body	**corpus, corporis (n)**
bold	**audax, audacis**
book	**liber, libri (m)**
both … and	**et … et**
boy	**puer, pueri (m)**
brave	**fortis, e**
bridge	**pons, pontis (m)**
brother	**frater, fratris (m)**
build, I	**aedifico (1)**
bull	**taurus (m)**
but	**sed**
call, I	**voco (1)**
camp	**castra, castrorum (n.pl)**
capture, I	**capio (3)**
carry, I	**porto (1)**
catch sight of, I	**conspicio (3)**
cavalry	**equites, equitum (m.pl)**
children	**pueri, puerorum (m.pl)**
citizen	**civis, civis, (m/f)**
city	**urbs, urbis (f)**
climb, I	**ascendo (3)**
come, I	**venio (4)**
companion	**comes, comitis (m/f)**
compel, I	**cogo (3)**
consul	**consul, consulis (m)**
couch, bed	**lectus, lecti (m)**
country(side)	**rus, ruris (n)**
country-house	**villa, villae (f)**
crowd	**turba, turbae (f)**
cruel	**crudelis, e**
cunning	**callidus, a, um**
danger	**periculum, periculi (n)**

daring	**audax, audacis**
daughter	**filia, filiae (f)**
day	**dies, diei (m)**
decide, I	**constituo (3)**
deep	**altus, a, um**
defeat, I	**vinco (3), supero (1)**
delay	**mora, morae (f)**
depart, I	**discedo (3)**
desire, I	**cupio (3)**
destroy, I	**deleo (2)**
difficult	**difficilis, e**
dining-room	**triclinium, triclinii (n)**
dinner	**cena, cenae (f)**
do, I	**facio (3)**
dog	**canis, canis (m/f)**
door	**ianua, ianuae (f)**
down from	**de + Abl**
drag, I	**traho (3)**
drive, I	**pello (3)**
easy	**facilis, e**
eight	**octo**
eighth	**octavus, a, um**
enemy	**hostis, hostis (m/f)**
enter, I	**intro (1)**
entrance-hall	**atrium, atrii (n)**
escape, I	**effugio (3)**
even	**etiam**
evening	**vesper, vesperi (m)**
every	**omnis, e**
eye	**oculus, oculi (m)**
faith	**fides, fidei (f)**
fall, I	**cado (3)**
far	**longe**
farmer	**agricola, agricolae (m)**
father	**pater, patris (m)**
fear, I	**timeo (2)**
field	**ager, agri (m)**
fierce	**ferox, ferocis**
	saevus, a, um

fifth	**quintus, a, um**
fight, I	**pugno (1)**
find, I	**invenio (4)**
fire	**ignis, ignis (m)**
first	**primus, a, um**
five	**quinque**
flee, I	**fugio (3)**
flock	**grex, gregis (m)**
flower	**flos, floris (m)**
food	**cibus, cibi (m)**
foot	**pes, pedis (m)**
for (because)	**enim**
for a long time	**diu**
forbid, I	**veto (1)**
force	**impetus, impetus (m)**
force, I	**cogo (3)**
forum	**forum, fori (n)**
four	**quattuor**
fourth	**quartus, a, um**
freedman	**libertus, liberti (m)**
friend	**amicus, amici (m)**
frighten, I	**terreo (2)**
from	**a, ab + Abl**
garden	**hortus, horti (m)**
girl	**puella, puellae (f)**
give, I	**do (1)**
give back, I	**reddo (3)**
go down, I	**descendo (3)**
god	**deus, dei (m)**
goddess	**dea, deae (f)**
gold	**aurum, auri (n)**
good	**bonus, a, um**
great	**magnus, a, um**
greet, I	**saluto (1)**
grieve, I	**doleo (2)**
guard	**custos, custodis (m/f)**
hand	**manus, manus (f)**
hand over, I	**trado (3)**

happy	**laetus, a, um**
harbour	**portus, portus (m)**
have, I	**habeo (2)**
head	**caput, capitis (n)**
hear, I	**audio (4)**
heaven	**caelum, caeli (n)**
heavy	**gravis, e**
hello!	**salve(te)**
help	**auxilium, auxilii (n)**
help, I	**iuvo (1)**
herd	**grex, gregis (m)**
here	**hic**
high	**altus, a, um**
himself/herself/themselves	**se**
his/her/its/their own	**suus, a, um**
hold, I	**teneo (2)**
home	**domus, domus (f)**
hope	**spes, spei (f)**
horse	**equus, equi (m)**
hot	**calidus, a, um**
house	**casa, casae (f)**
how many?	**quot?**
however	**tamen**
huge	**ingens, ingentis**
hurry, I	**festino (1)**
husband	**vir, viri (m)**
I	**ego**
immediately	**statim**
in	**in + Abl**
inhabitant	**incola, incolae, (m/f)**
into	**in + Acc**
island	**insula, insulae (f)**
journey	**iter, itineris (n)**
keep safe, I	**servo (1), conservo (1)**
kill, I	**neco (1), occido (3)**
king	**rex, regis (m)**
kitchen	**culina, culinae (f)**

knee	**genu, genus (n)**
know, I	**scio (4)**
know, I do not	**nescio (4)**
large	**magnus, a, um**
lead, I	**duco (3)**
leader, chief, emperor	**princeps, principis (m)**
leader, guide	**dux, ducis (m/f)**
leave, I	**discedo (3)**
letter	**epistola, epistolae (f)**
lie down, I	**iaceo (2)**
light	**lux, lucis (f)**
like, I	**amo (1)**
lion	**leo, leonis (m)**
listen to, I	**audio (4)**
little	**parvus, a, um**
live in, I	**habito (1)**
long	**longus, a, um**
look!	**ecce**
look after, I	**curo (1)**
look at, I	**specto (1)**
love, I	**amo (1)**
lucky	**felix, felicis**
make, I	**facio (3)**
man	**vir, viri (m)**
many	**multi, ae, a**
marriage	**matrimonium, matrimonii (n)**
master	**dominus, domini (m)**
message	**nuntius, nuntii (m)**
messenger	**nuntius, nuntii (m)**
midday	**meridies, meridiei (m)**
miserable	**miser, era, erum**
money	**pecunia, pecuniae (f)**
moon	**luna, lunae (f)**
mother	**mater, matris (f)**
mountain	**mons, montis (m)**
move, I	**moveo (2)**
must, I	**debeo (2)**
my	**meus, a, um**

near	**prope + Acc**
neither ... nor	**neque ... neque**
new	**novus, a, um**
night	**nox, noctis (f)**
nine	**novem**
ninth	**nonus, a, um**
not	**non**
nothing	**nihil**
now	**nunc, iam**
obey, I	**pareo (2) + Dat**
often	**saepe**
old, ancient	**antiquus, a, um**
old man	**senes, senis (m)**
on	**in + Abl**
on account of	**propter + Acc**
on behalf of	**pro + Abl**
on to	**in + Acc**
one	**unus, a, um**
order, I	**iubeo (2)**
ought to, I	**debeo (2)**
our	**noster, tra, trum**
out of	**e, ex + Abl**
over, on top of	**super + Acc**
overcome, I	**supero (1), vinco (3)**
own country/city	**patria, patriae (f)**
part	**pars, partis (f)**
place, I	**pono (3)**
play, I	**ludo (3)**
please, I	**placeo (2) + Dat**
poem	**carmen, carminis (n)**
poet	**poeta, poetae (m)**
point out, I	**monstro (1)**
praise, I	**laudo (1)**
prepare, I	**paro (1)**
put, I	**pono (3)**
queen	**regina, reginae (f)**
quickly	**celeriter**

race, tribe, family	**gens, gentis (f)**
read, I	**lego (3)**
reply, I	**respondeo (2)**
river	**flumen, fluminis (n)**
river-bank	**ripa, ripae (f)**
road	**via, viae (f)**
rock	**saxum, saxi (n)**
rule, I	**rego (3)**
run, I	**curro (3)**
run away, I	**fugio (3)**
safe	**tutus, a, um**
sail, I	**navigo (1)**
sailor	**nauta, nautae (f)**
sand	**arena, arenae (f)**
say, I	**dico (3)**
school	**ludus, ludi (m)**
schoolmaster	**magister, magistri (m)**
sea	**mare, maris (n)**
second	**secundus, a, um**
see, I	**video (2)**
seek, I	**peto (3)**
seize, I	**occupo (1)**
senate	**senatus, senatus (m)**
senator	**senator, senatoris (m)**
send, I	**mitto (3)**
serious	**gravis, e**
seven	**septem**
seventh	**septimus, a, um**
shade	**umbra, umbrae (f)**
ship	**navis, navis (f)**
shore	**ora, orae (f)**
short	**brevis, e**
shout	**clamor, clamoris (m)**
shout, I	**clamo (1)**
show, I	**monstro (1), ostendo (3)**
signal	**signum, signi (n)**
silent, I am	**taceo (2)**
sing, I	**canto (1)**
sister	**soror, sororis (f)**

sit, I	**sedeo (2)**
six	**sex**
sixth	**sextus, a, um**
sky	**caelum, caeli (n)**
slave	**servus, servi (m)**
sleep	**somnus, somni (m)**
sleep, I	**dormio (4)**
slowly	**lente**
small	**parvus, a, um**
so, such	**tam**
soldier	**miles, militis (m/f)**
song	**carmen, carminis (n)**
soon	**mox**
speak, I	**dico (3)**
spear	**hasta, hastae (f)**
stand, I	**sto (1)**
stay, I	**maneo (2)**
step	**gradus, gradus (m)**
stone	**saxum, saxi (n)**
storm	**tempestas, tempestatis (f)**
story	**fabula, fabulae (f)**
strong	**validus, a, um**
suddenly	**subito**
sun	**sol, solis (m)**
surely not?	**num?**
surely?	**nonne?**
swim, I	**nato (1)**
sweet	**dulcis, e**
sword	**gladius (m)**
table	**mensa, mensae (f)**
teach, I	**doceo (2)**
tell, I	**dico (3)**
tell (a story), I	**narro (1)**
temple	**templum, templi (n)**
ten	**decem**
tenth	**decimus, a, um**
the other (of two)	**alter, era, erum**
theatre	**theatrum, theatri (n)**
then	**deinde**

there	**ibi**
therefore	**igitur, itaque**
thing, affair, matter, event	**res, rei (f)**
third	**tertius, a, um**
three	**tres**
through	**per + Acc**
throw, I	**iacio (3)**
time	**tempus, temporis (n)**
tired	**fessus, a, um**
to, towards	**ad + Acc**
today	**hodie**
tomorrow	**cras**
town	**oppidum, oppidi (n)**
tree	**arbor, arboris (f)**
two	**duo**
us	**nos**
very (much)	**valde**
voice	**vox, vocis (f)**
wait, I	**maneo (2)**
wait for, I	**exspecto (1)**
wall	**murus, muri (m)**
walk, I	**ambulo (1)**
wander, I	**erro (1)**
want, I	**cupio (3)**
war	**bellum, belli (n)**
warn, I	**moneo (2)**
water	**aqua, aquae (f)**
wave	**unda, undae (f)**
we	**nos**
weapon	**telum, teli (n)**
weep, I	**fleo (2)**
well	**bene**
what?	**quid?**
what kind of?	**qualis, e?**
where?	**ubi?**
who?	**quis?**
why?	**cur?**

wife	**uxor, uxoris**
wind	**ventus, venti (m)**
wine	**vinum, vini (n)**
wise	**sapiens, sapientis**
wish, I	**cupio (3)**
with	**cum + Abl**
without	**sine + Abl**
woman	**femina, feminae (f)**
	mulier, mulieris (f)
wood	**silva, silvae (f)**
word	**verbum, verbi (n)**
work, I	**laboro (1)**
wound	**vulnus, vulneris (n)**
wound, I	**vulnero (1)**
wretched	**miser, era, erum**
writing-tablet	**tabula, tabulae (f)**
year	**annus, anni (m)**
you (plural)	**vester, tra, trum**
you (singular)	**tu**
young man	**iuvenis, iuvenis (m)**
your (plural)	**vos**
your (sing)	**tuus, a, um**